# THE NUTS AND BOLTS OF ENGLISH GRAMMAR

D1707967

# THE NUTS AND BOLTS OF ENGLISH GRAMMAR

NORHAIDA AMAN • LUDWIG TAN

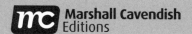

**Marshall Cavendish**
Editions

© 2018 Marshall Cavendish International (Asia) Private Limited
Text © Norhaida Aman and Ludwig Tan
All illustrations by Hasyim Isa and Nursyazwani Ghazali

Reprinted 2018, 2019

Published by Marshall Cavendish Editions
An imprint of Marshall Cavendish International

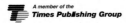

Other Marshall Cavendish Offices:
Marshall Cavendish Corporation, 99 White Plains Road, Tarrytown NY 10591-9001, USA
• Marshall Cavendish International (Thailand) Co Ltd, 253 Asoke, 12th Flr, Sukhumvit 21
Road, Klongtoey Nua, Wattana, Bangkok 10110, Thailand • Marshall Cavendish (Malaysia)
Sdn Bhd, Times Subang, Lot 46, Subang Hi-Tech Industrial Park, Batu Tiga, 40000 Shah
Alam, Selangor Darul Ehsan, Malaysia.

**National Library Board, Singapore Cataloguing-in-Publication Data**

Name(s): Norhaida Aman. | Tan, Ludwig, author. | Hasyim Isa, illustrator. |
Nursyazwani Ghazali, illustrator.
Title: The nuts and bolts of English grammar / Norhaida Aman, Ludwig Tan ; all
illustrations by Hasyim Isa and Nursyazwani Ghazali.
Description: Singapore : Marshall Cavendish Editions, [2018]
Identifier(s): OCN 1015222349 | ISBN 978-981-47-7139-9
Subject(s): LCSH: English language--Grammar.
Classification: DDC 428.2--dc23

Printed in Singapore

*For our NIE and SUSS students,*
*both past and present,*
*who have been some of our best teachers*

# Contents

# Preface

*The Nuts and Bolts of English Grammar* has a simple aim: to explain how the grammar of English works, in language as simple as possible. Hence, it has been written with a wide audience in mind, including students of English, trainee teachers, and even the general reader – such as parents – who does not have a background in English grammar, yet wishes to know how it works.

In this book, we take you on a journey through English grammar, beginning with the nuts and bolts of the English language – the word, as well as units smaller than the word called "morphemes" – and progressing to phrases, clauses and, finally, sentences. Chapter 1 briefly discusses what "grammar" means and how grammarians study language. In Chapter 2, we examine word class and how we go about deciding what word class a word belongs to. In Chapters 3 and 4, we take a look at nouns and verbs, and how they may be expanded to form noun phrases and verb phrases. In Chapter 5, we explore how phrases may be combined in various ways to form clauses and sentences, and in Chapter 6, we look at the different ways in which sentences may be structured. We then move beyond the level of the sentence and look at the finer points of writing, such as subject-verb agreement in Chapter 7 and punctuation in Chapter 8.

When we began exploring the idea of writing a grammar book, we decided that it had to be easy enough to be read, from cover to cover, by someone with little or no background in English grammar. Yet, we also wanted it to meet the practical needs of students of grammar, as well as teachers and parents. We felt that, with almost 30 years of teaching experience between us, we were well placed to do this. As teachers of undergraduate students and trainee teachers, we have both accumulated a vast trove of grammar-related examples and puzzles, some of which have been incorporated into this book in the form of examples in the text. In addition, they may be found in the Grammar Detective puzzles, which are short exercises that get you to apply what you've just learnt to common issues in English grammar. Instead of ramming technical terms – of which there are many in grammar! – down the reader's throat, we have tried to demystify them by breaking them down and explaining what they mean. To keep this book accessible to the general reader, we have deliberately kept this book fairly simple in its coverage, so it does not contain exhaustive lists of determiners, irregular verbs and suchlike. However, by the end of this book, you should have become sufficiently familiar with grammatical terms and concepts to be able to consult reference grammars such as *Practical English Usage* (by Michael Swan; Oxford University Press) and the *Cambridge Grammar of English* (by Ronald Carter & Michael McCarthy; Cambridge University Press).

## Acknowledgements

Writing a book is never easy, and the gestation of this book was anything but smooth. This book has been two years in the making. During this time, we've been able to count on She-reen Wong, our excellent editor at Marshall Cavendish, for her infinite patience, especially when draft chapters were slow to appear. We've benefited greatly from her meticulous attention to detail and valuable insights into language and publishing, which have made our manuscript come to life, resulting in a book that is, we hope, better than it might otherwise have been. To her, we owe a huge debt of thanks and gratitude. We would also like to acknowledge the help given to us by Lee Mei Lin, especially when the book was at the proposal stage.

    We would also like to thank our families for their support and patience during the past two years. Without them, this book would never have seen the light of day.

*Norhaida Aman and Ludwig Tan*
*December 2017*

# About the Authors

**Dr Norhaida Aman** is lecturer and programme leader of English Language and Literature at the National Institute of Education, Singapore (NIE). She holds a PhD from the University of Delaware, USA. She is a linguist and teacher educator specialising in grammar and language acquisition; almost half of her life has been dedicated to teaching and serving current and future generations. She teaches grammar across all programmes at NIE, and also courses on language acquisition. Over the years, she has established strategic partnerships with various agencies: Ministry of Education, Singapore, local and international schools, government agencies and academics. These collaborations, together with her teaching and research interests, have allowed her to impact teacher education and pre-school education both locally and abroad.

**Associate Professor Ludwig Tan** is Vice Dean of the School of Arts & Social Sciences at the Singapore University of Social Sciences (SUSS). He holds a PhD and MPhil (Linguistics) from the University of Cambridge, and a BA (First-Class Honours) in English Language and Linguistics from Lancaster University, UK. A linguist and a trained teacher, he has worked as a teacher educator at the National Institute of Education (NIE), Singapore, and served as a consultant to the Ministry of Education on its 2010 English Language Syllabus. At SUSS, he teaches courses on grammar, phonetics and Singapore English. He is a steering committee member of the Speak Good English Movement, and co-author, with Alvin Leong, of *English Grammar FAQs: 100 Questions Teachers and Students Frequently Ask* (McGraw-Hill, 2008).

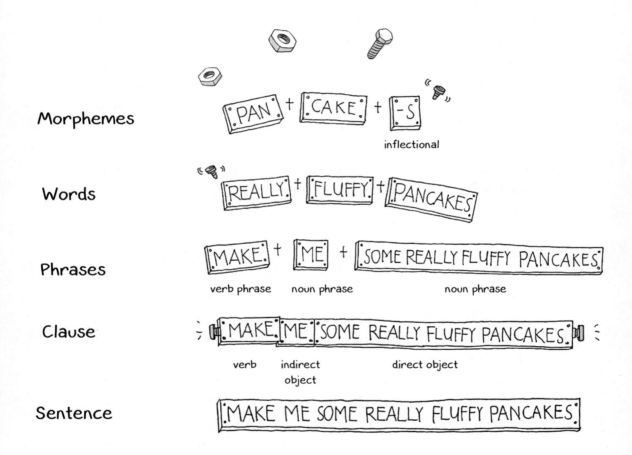

**Morphemes**

PAN + CAKE + -S
*inflectional*

**Words**

REALLY + FLUFFY + PANCAKES

**Phrases**

MAKE + ME + SOME REALLY FLUFFY PANCAKES
*verb phrase*    *noun phrase*       *noun phrase*

**Clause**

MAKE ME SOME REALLY FLUFFY PANCAKES
*verb*    *indirect*      *direct object*
        *object*

**Sentence**

MAKE ME SOME REALLY FLUFFY PANCAKES

# CHAPTER ONE

# INTRODUCTION

Have you ever wondered why we can say *Maria made the boy cry*, but not *Maria made the boy crying*?

Or why *Two coffees, please* is acceptable, but *Melvin loves coffees* is generally wrong?

Or why we say *It has been raining since ten*, even though we cannot ask *What did you say has been raining*?

These are some of the kinds of puzzles we will be examining in **The Nuts and Bolts of English Grammar**. As the title suggests, the main purpose of this book is to help you understand what English grammar is and how it works. We hope you'll find this book useful, whether you've purchased it for a course or are simply curious about the ways in which English grammar functions.

## What is Grammar?

The word *grammar* can be used in three different ways. Have a look at the following sentences and ask yourself what the word means in each one of them:

1. *The grammar of Tamil is very different from that of English.*
2. *I've just read Kevin's letter and his grammar is atrocious!*
3. *The linguists are writing a new reference grammar of English.*

You'll have noticed that, in each of the above sentences, the word *grammar* has a different sense, or meaning. In sentence 1, *grammar* refers to "the rules in a language for changing the form of words and joining them into sentences" (*Oxford Advanced Learner's Dictionary*, 2005:675); in other words, Tamil and English are very different in how they string words together to form sentences. By contrast, the word *grammar* in sentence 2 refers to a person's command of the rules of a language – hence, we learn that Kevin's grammar isn't very good, meaning he probably puts words in the wrong order, or doesn't put an *-s* at the end of verbs and nouns when he needs to. Finally, sentence 3 tells us that linguists are putting together a reference work that lays out the rules of English grammar, just as a dictionary tries to record and explain all the words currently in use in a language.

Clearly, it's the sense in sentence 1 that this book is concerned with. We will, as we work through this book, be finding out how English combines parts of words such as stems and suffixes to form longer words, how words change their forms to show grammatical information such as tense and number, how words then combine with other words to form phrases, and how phrases are subsequently combined to form clauses and sentences, and larger units such as texts.

## What Grammar is Not

If you've grown up in Singapore, you would probably have learnt at least two languages when you were in school. You may also have heard people make such claims like *English has grammar; Chinese doesn't.* However, this is based on the misconception that grammar involves only word endings or inflections such as *-s*, *-ed* and *-en*, which exist in English to show grammatical information such as tense, aspect and number. (Do not worry about these terms for now as we will examine them in later chapters.) Rather, as we briefly saw above, grammar refers to the *structure* of a language. If indeed Chinese did not have any grammar, then how do its billions of speakers understand each other? Clearly, in Chinese there is a more or less fixed order of subject, verb, object, etc. In other words, it has structural rules that its speakers follow and observe, so that when they speak the language, they understand each other.

Similarly, you may have heard the claim that Singlish – or to give its technical name, Colloquial Singapore English (CSE) – has no grammar, or that it should be regarded simply as bad or ungrammatical English. However, imagine that you have a new neighbour who has recently moved to Singapore and is keen to fit in by learning the local lingo. You've taught him a few words of Singlish, and one day, feeling supremely confident, he asks you, *You already eat?* You'll probably think it sounds vaguely Singlish, but there's still something not quite right about it. Upon reflection, you realise he was right to leave *eat* unconjugated, or not marked for tense (e.g. into the past tense *ate*), but what he said sounded strange because he placed *already* before the verb *eat*. What this shows is that Singlish DOES have grammar – that is, it has rules governing where words are placed in a sentence. If Singlish didn't have grammar, then *Already you eat?* and *Eat you already?* would both be possible – but these are ungrammatical in Singlish.

## Why Study Grammar?

If you have unpleasant memories of studying grammar in English class in primary and secondary school, you're not alone. Admittedly, grammar *can* be very dry, especially if you are or were studying it solely to pass exams.

However, it can be very fascinating and useful to explore and apply to authentic examples. In this book, we hope to make grammar both interesting and practical by getting you to apply concepts that we've just discussed to real-life grammar puzzles, such as the ones that opened this chapter. Will this book help you to improve your grammar (that's the sense of the word illustrated in sentence 2 above), however? The answer is "probably", because if you've gained a better understanding of grammar by the time you reach the end of this book, you should be able to analyse your own sentences in ways you've never done before, and spot and avoid common grammatical errors.

## Approaches to Studying Grammar

Before we begin delving into the study of grammar, let's take a look at two main ways in which grammar is studied by grammarians – that is, people who study the grammar of languages.

First, there are **prescriptive grammarians**, who see grammar rules as a code of behaviour to be followed by speakers. As the term implies, prescriptive grammarians *prescribe* grammar rules to users of the language, just as doctors prescribe medicine to patients. While some of these rules are indeed essential to the language, many of them are not in fact followed by normal speakers in normal situations, or have no grammatical basis. Prescriptive grammarians also tend to believe that new developments in a language are bad and lead to the decay of the language. They label speakers' use of language as either good or bad. The approach to language study that prescriptive grammarians follow is called *prescriptivism*.

By contrast, **descriptive grammarians** are primarily interested in describing how language is used by speakers of a language at any point in its history. They form rules of grammar by observing what real speakers of the language actually say. New developments in a language do not upset descriptive grammarians; in fact most of them find it exciting to study new patterns of usage in a language and do not lament that the language is going to the dogs. Descriptive grammarians label speakers' use of language as either grammatical or ungrammatical, and the approach they follow is called *descriptivism*.

To illustrate the difference between prescriptive and descriptive grammarians, let us take a look at the following sentences:

4.   *Who did she send the letter to?*
5.   *To whom did she send the letter?*
6.   *\*Who she did send the letter to?*

Now, which sentence are you most likely to say? If you're like most people, you'd probably find sentence 4 the most natural. Sentence 5 might be acceptable to you if you heard or read it, but you would most probably not use it yourself. As for 6, this probably sounds very odd to you, and if you did hear it, you would wonder if the speaker was a learner of English.

Now, how about grammarians – what would they think of these sentences? Let's start with sentence 4: if you were to ask a descriptive grammarian, he or she would say that it is *grammatical* because it would be uttered by normal, fluent speakers in real life, such as yourself. However, a prescriptive grammarian would say that 4 is bad because the question ends with a preposition, and that *whom* should be used instead of *who* as the recipient is the object of the preposition. Hence, the prescriptive grammarian might offer sentence 5 as an alternative that is good – however, the descriptive grammarian would note that while it is not ungrammatical, it is very formal indeed, and more suitable in writing rather than speech. As for sentence 6, both prescriptive and descriptive grammarians would agree that it is ungrammatical as it does not follow the normal English **word order** – or order in which words appear in a sentence – and would not be uttered by a competent speaker of the language. Notice that it has been starred, or marked with an asterisk – in linguistics, this means that it is ungrammatical or poorly formed, and not that it is excellent!

## Variation in English

You will probably have noticed that you don't speak the same way all the time – rather, you vary the way you speak depending on whom you're talking to and the situation you're in, most of the time without even realising it.

Our use of language may change according to situation – whether we are speaking or writing, what kind of text or conversation or speech we are producing, how formal or informal the event or text is, and whom we are talking to or being read by. This leads us to write or speak in a certain **register**, or very roughly, language style. The speaking style we use when catching up with friends would be very different from that used by a minister launching a major policy as both situations are polar opposites in terms of **formality**: a meet-up with friends is highly informal, whereas a ministerial launch event is usually highly formal. Accordingly, speakers in both situations would use very different **linguistic features**, such as vocabulary. For example, you and your friends might describe your meeting up as *awesome*, but the minister might describe the launch event as *splendid*. Register also very much depends on whether the communication is written or spoken. Writing is generally more formal than speaking – for example, the language in a press release at an event at which a minister announces a new policy will be a lot more formal and standard than the conversations journalists may have during the tea break.

Language can vary according to **language variety**. In Singapore, language choice may vary between Standard English – which is a formal, internationally understood variety of English – and Colloquial Singapore English, or to use the more familiar term, Singlish – which is mainly spoken among family and friends in informal situations.

Hence, when we encounter an instance of language use, apart from judging it merely as grammatical or ungrammatical, we should also consider the context in which it appears. For example, when we see Singlish in public signs, what makes this unusual is not that Singlish is ungrammatical, but because it is arguably out of place in a formal, official context where we would expect Standard English to be used instead. Likewise, if a writer uses contractions such as *don't* and *can't* in a formal report, this may attract disapproval not because contractions are ungrammatical – they aren't – but because their use is primarily associated with informal contexts.

## Overview of Grammar

In this book, we'll be looking at the nuts and bolts of English grammar such as roots and suffixes, before moving on to larger units such as clauses and sentences. Let's illustrate this with the following sentence:

7.   *Make me some really fluffy pancakes!*

There are several levels at which we can analyse the utterance above.

First, we can look at how words are formed: for example, the word *pancakes* has three parts, or three **morphemes**: the root words *pan* and *cake* and the plural suffix *-s*.

Next, we can then look at all the parts of a sentence at word level and ask ourselves what **word class** each word belongs to. So, *make* is a verb, *me* is a pronoun, *some* is a determiner, *really* is an adverb, *fluffy* is an adjective, and finally, *pancakes* is a noun.

Moving on, we can look at how words are combined to form **phrases**. In the above sentence we have the noun phrase *really fluffy pancakes*, which we understand to be about the noun *pancakes*. Additionally, the adjective phrase *really fluffy* (itself formed from the adjective *fluffy*, with the adverb *really* telling us how fluffy) describes what the pancakes are like.

The next level up is the **clause**, which is built around the verb: the verb tells us what is happening and who the participants are and what they're doing. Here, we have *make* as the verb, and we note that there are two participants mentioned: the direct object *really fluffy pancakes*, and the indirect object *me*, which is the recipient. So the clause has the structure: verb + indirect object + direct object.

Finally, we can look at the utterance above and ask ourselves what its **form** and **function** are. In terms of form – or what the utterance looks like – the utterance is an imperative, meaning that it has a verb and other parts of the clause, but no subject. In terms of function, however, it is a directive, i.e. its purpose is to direct someone to do something.

## Conclusion

We began this chapter by looking at definitions of grammar and approaches to studying the grammar of languages – namely, the prescriptive and descriptive approaches. We also looked at how the use of English, and indeed any other language, varies according to context. Finally, we took a quick look at the kinds of grammatical analysis we will be engaging in later in this book.

### *Grammar Detective*

Think back to your school days. Were you ever told by your teachers that it was wrong to begin sentences with conjunctions such as *and* and *because*? Do you still follow that rule, and do you think it's truly ungrammatical to begin a sentence with *and* or *because*? Do you think this rule is a descriptive or a prescriptive one?

CHAPTER TWO

# WORD CLASS

In Chapter 1, we took a brief look at what grammar is and how grammarians study it. In this chapter, we'll focus on the nuts and bolts of sentences – the word. Specifically, we'll be studying word class, that is, looking at words and exploring how we can determine if they're nouns, adjectives, adverbs, prepositions, and so on.

## Why Study Word Class?

Being able to determine word class can be a very useful skill. It can help us understand the structure of phrases and sentences better. A very practical use for this is when we need to explain learners' errors: for example, if a friend who is learning English as a foreign language says to you, *Today is an excitement day*, you can explain to him that his sentence is wrong because, rather than using the noun *excitement*, he needs to use the adjective *exciting* to describe the word *day*, i.e. *Today is an exciting day*. Furthermore, understanding what word class is about is essential when we're learning a new word: apart from knowing its meaning, we need to know what class of word (e.g. is it an adjective or a noun?) it belongs to in order to use it correctly.

## Words and Morphemes

What's the smallest unit of a sentence? If you ask any of your friends — especially those who haven't studied English or any other language in a technical way before — they're likely to answer "word".

However, as we saw in Chapter 1, a word such as *bookmarks* can be broken up into three different parts: *book*, *mark* and *-s*. The first two units, *book* and *mark*, are nouns and they combine to convey the meaning of a decorative piece of paper to mark a page in a book you're reading, or a web page you want to remember as you might be returning to it often, while the suffix *-s* indicates that there are two or more bookmarks. As we've just seen, each of the three parts of this word carries lexical or grammatical meaning. Linguists call these meaningful units, or building blocks of words, **morphemes**.

## Approach to Studying Word Class

We may classify words and assign them word class labels by looking at their meaning as well as how they behave in terms of grammar. In this book, we will be looking at the following eight major word classes: nouns, verbs, adjectives, pronouns, determiners, adverbs, prepositions, and conjunctions. In addition, we will be looking at minor word class labels such as infinitives, interjections and particles.

In addition to word class, you may also have heard of the term *parts of speech*. Both terms actually refer to the same thing; however, *parts of speech* is rather old-fashioned nowadays and would probably be familiar to older Singaporeans who attended English-medium schools.

## Meaning, Form and Function

When we look at a word and try to decide what its word class is, we can rely on three important clues: meaning, form and function.

**Meaning** is perhaps the one we turn to first: for example, when we see the word *pen*, we know that it refers to, or means, a writing instrument that lays a trail of ink on paper, hence it is probably a noun as it is a thing.

What about *pens*? At first glance, this looks like a noun in the plural form, because *pen* is a singular noun, and the plural suffix -*s* indicates that there is more than one pen. This is **form**: the "shape" of a word, or what it *looks* like. However, you may also have noticed that *pen* and *pens* may describe an action too: that of writing something down, usually with a pen, such as to "pen down your thoughts" or "pen a novel". Indeed, there are other related verb forms, such as *penned* and *penning*.

This brings us to **function**, or what a word is doing in a constituent (that is, a unit of grammar that may stand on its own) such as a phrase or a clause. In the phrase *a green pen*, for example, the word *pen* acts, or *functions*, as the head of the noun phrase, which also has premodifiers in the form of the determiner *the* and the adjective *green*. (Terms such as noun phrases and premodifiers will be covered in Chapter 3.) Hence, *pen* is a noun in the noun phrase. In the sentence *The newly retired diplomat will pen his memoirs soon*, however, *pen* tells us what action the diplomat is engaged in, hence it functions as the verb of the clause.

Therefore, when determining the word class of any word, remember that you cannot always tell what class a word belongs to just by looking at its meaning or form. Rather, you need to consider meaning, form and function before you can assign a word-class label to the word.

Let's now take a quick look at a sentence so that we can understand better what word class is about:

1. *That young but experienced chef cooked a really superb pizza for me yesterday.*

Let's begin with the nouns: *chef* and *pizza* are nouns as they are names for people and things. The words *young* and *experienced* are adjectives as they describe *chef*. Another adjective is *superb*, which describes *pizza*. Then we have *that*, which helps point out or determine the chef we are talking about, hence it is a determiner, and so is *a*, which refers to the pizza. The word *me* is a pronoun; it refers to the speaker and saves him or her from having to mention his or her name and possibly causing confusion. Then we have *but*, a conjunction which joins the adjectives *new* and *experienced*, and suggests that it's a somewhat unexpected combination (i.e. experienced chefs tend to be older). Then we have *cooked*, which is a verb and tells us what happened, i.e. what the chef did to the pizza. Next, we have *really* and *yesterday*, which are adverbs: *yesterday* tells us when the chef cooked the pizza for me, and *really* tells us how superb it was. Finally, we have *for*, which is a preposition, and tells the reader that the recipient of the pizza was *me*.

We'll very shortly take a closer look at each word class. Before we begin, we'll discuss briefly what content words and function words are. **Content words** are those with semantic content, i.e. are heavy in meaning, whereas **function words** exist mainly to convey grammatical information. Hence, adjectives, nouns and many adverbs are content words, whereas prepositions, determiners and conjunctions are function words.

A concept that is closely related to this is the distinction between open-class and closed-class words. An **open class** of words is one that accepts new words readily; in this class, we have adjectives and nouns – because new words have to be coined to describe new things, feelings and so on. By contrast, a **closed class** of words is one that does not, or does not easily, admit of new members. This includes prepositions, determiners and conjunctions, because these have very limited functions and had already been thought of a long time ago. Adverbs, of course, contain a very wide range of words, some of them closed-class (e.g. *here, now, not, more, less*) and others open-class (e.g. *slowly, interestingly, surprisingly*). We will examine this more closely when we explore each of the eight major word classes below.

## Nouns

We'll explore word class by first looking at **nouns**. After all, nouns are the first words that infants utter because nouns are names of things and people. It is only natural that an infant who begins talking wants to name things he or she can see around him or her, such as *Mama, Papa, cat* and *car*.

The word *noun* comes from the Latin *nomen*, meaning "name"; as we'd expect, nouns name people (e.g. *woman, accountant, electrician, writer, Paul, president*), animals (e.g. *squirrel, viper, sandpiper, alligator*), things (e.g. *shelf, luggage, apartment, canister, temple, ruins*), places (e.g. *home, Singapore, Kazakhstan, Nigeria, Greece, New Zealand*), and ideas and actions (e.g. *happiness, peace, optimism, creativity, swimming, dancing*).

Many nouns have typical noun suffixes or endings, such as *-er, -ation, -ity* and *-ness*, especially if they are derived or formed from words of other classes, such as verbs and adjectives. These suffixes make such nouns instantly recognised by their form alone. In addition, nouns may end in *-s* to show that they're plural.

A large number of nouns also end in *-ing* because they are derived from the progressive *-ing* participles of verbs, and hence typically name activities. Such nouns are called **gerunds**, and typical examples of these include *walking, cycling, swimming, driving* and *reading*. Usually, it is easy to tell whether an *-ing* word is a verb or a gerund (noun). Consider the following sentences:

2.   *I love cycling in the rain.*
3.   *I love cycling.*

In the first sentence, the word *cycling* is best analysed as a verb as it tells us about the speaker *doing* something in the rain. In the second, however, the speaker is just naming an activity he or she loves, hence it's more logical to think of *cycling* as a gerund, that is, a noun in the *-ing* form. One way to show that it is indeed a noun is to replace it with a pronoun, i.e. *I love it.* By comparison, note that we cannot do it with the earlier sentence, *\*I love it in the rain* – this shows that we have to take *cycling* together with *in the rain* as a constituent or grammatical unit (as we shall see in later chapters, this is a non-finite clause functioning like a noun).

Nouns are open-class words as new words need to be invented to name new ideas, inventions, activities, places and so on. We'll take a much closer look at nouns and noun phrases in Chapter 3.

## Verbs

Imagine that we're trying to tell a story, and the only words we know are nouns. We probably wouldn't get very far because, apart from being able to name the people and things involved, we would not be able to say what they are doing, feeling or saying, or indeed, what is happening.

This is where **verbs** come in. Verbs are words that describe actions (e.g. *write, play, forgive, tell, run*) and states and processes (e.g. *be, know, understand, live, love, miss, freeze, melt*). Verbs can often be recognised by their form: they're the words with endings such as the *-s* third-person singular present tense marker, the *-(e)d* past tense marker, and the *-ed/en* and *-ing* participles, giving us verb forms such as *plays, melted, frozen* and *freezing.* Apart from these main verbs, which carry meaning and tell us what is happening in a sentence, there are also auxiliary verbs, which convey grammatical information such as whether an action is deemed to be completed or ongoing. In the sentence *The kids have been crying all day*, we have a verb group made up of the main verb *crying*, which tells us what the kids did, and auxiliary verbs *have* and *been*, which tell us that they are crying at the moment of speaking, and had begun doing so some time ago.

Verbs are open-class words as new verbs have to be created to describe new actions or even ways of thinking, living and speaking – for example the verbs *facepalm, friendzone* and *dox,* which may not even be found in dictionaries published in the last few years.

Before we move on to adjectives, note that a great many verbs and nouns have identical forms. For example, the words *drive, say* and *swim* are verbs in *I can <u>drive</u>, They <u>say</u> they're reliable* and *We <u>swim</u> every morning,* but they are nouns in *I enjoy a long <u>drive</u>, She doesn't have a <u>say</u> in these matters,* and *He had a relaxing <u>swim</u> this evening.* Furthermore, some verb and noun suffixes are identical too, e.g. the *-s* plural marker on nouns and the *-s* present tense marker on verbs, as well as the *-ing* suffix on verbs and on gerunds (nouns). Therefore, when deciding what word class a word falls under, we need to look beyond meaning and form, and also look at function.

## Adjectives

Imagine that you're reading a story that contains only nouns and verbs. So, although you know who the characters are in the story, and what they're doing or saying, you have no idea about their appearance or personalities. This is where **adjectives** come in. Simply put, they are describing words, and they exist to describe people, things, ideas, actions, events, feelings, and so on.

Since adjectives belong to an open class of words, there are countless adjectives in English (or indeed any other language) and they include words such as *happy, exciting, fascinated, repulsive, commendable, curious* and *historic*.

Most adjectives appear in either of two main positions: before a noun, and after a linking verb (a verb that equates a subject to its description). If we wish to describe a student as *brilliant*, for example, we can do so in either of these two ways:

4. *a <u>brilliant</u> student*  (before a noun)
5. *The student is <u>brilliant</u>.*  (after a linking verb)

Some adjectives may even come after a noun, within the noun phrase (more about this in Chapter 3). Let's take the adjective *united*. As the following examples show, *united* can appear in any of three positions:

6.  *a <u>united</u> country  (before the noun)*
7.  *a country <u>united</u>  (after the noun)*
8.  *The country is <u>united</u>.  (after a linking verb)*

However, this is by no means common among adjectives: only a small number of them out of thousands in the English language may follow the noun. Most are like *superb* and *brilliant*, which can be placed only before nouns, so we cannot say \**an idea superb* or \**a student brilliant*.

Adjectives may come in more than one form. The adjective *big*, for example, has three forms: *big, bigger, biggest*. The first form, *big*, is called the **base** form, and is used when we are making a simple description. However, when we are comparing two things, we use the **comparative** form, *bigger*, with the suffix *-er*; and when we want to say that something is the ultimate compared to the rest, we use the **superlative** form, *biggest*, with the suffix *-est*. These are said to be **regular** comparative and superlative forms, and are summarised below:

9.  *Rina lives in a <u>big</u> house.  (base)*
10. *Mani's house is <u>bigger</u>.  (comparative)*
11. *However, Abdul's house is the <u>biggest</u>.  (superlative)*

Although many adjectives that are one or two syllables long form the comparative and superlative forms by adding the suffixes *-er* and *-est*, many form them by using *more* and *most* respectively, e.g. *more useful, most useful* (rather than \**usefuller* and \**usefullest*).

There are also a great many adjectives whose comparative and superlative forms are **irregular**, meaning that they do not simply add *-er* or *-est*. Take *good, better* and *best*, for example: although they are all different forms of the same basic adjective, they do not bear even a superficial resemblance.

**Grammar Detective**

Is there anything wrong with the sentence below?

*I am the worse cook among the three of us.*

Adjectives may sometimes look like verbs, and this is because many adjectives were derived from the participle forms of verbs a long time ago. Have a look at the following sentences:

12. *Peter <u>inspired</u> us with his talk.*
13. *The students felt <u>inspired</u> after hearing him speak.*
14. *Peter is <u>inspiring</u> many students with his community work.*
15. *Peter is an <u>inspiring</u> social worker.*

In sentences 12 and 14, the words *inspired* and *inspiring* tell us what Peter is *doing*, which makes them verbs. In sentence 13, however, *inspired* describes the students, and in sentence 15, *inspiring* describes Peter – hence, they are *adjectives*. Incidentally, where there are pairs of adjectives in the *-ed* and *-ing* forms, the ones ending in *-ed* describe the subject (the students are inspired), whereas the ones ending in *-ing* describe the effect the subject has on others (Peter has the effect of inspiring others).

If you are unsure whether an *-ed/-ing* word is a verb or an adjective, the simplest test to try would be the "very" test:

16. *\*Peter very <u>inspired</u> us with his talk.*
17. *The students felt very <u>inspired</u> after hearing him speak.*
18. *\*Peter is very <u>inspiring</u> many students with his community work.*
19. *Peter is a very <u>inspiring</u> social worker.*

As we can see above, adding *very* results in ungrammatical sentences in 16 and 18, as marked by the asterisks, as *very* cannot be used to intensify actions. By contrast, sentences 17 and 19 are grammatical as the adverb *very* may intensify the adjectives *inspired* and *inspiring* to tell us how inspired the students felt, or how inspiring Peter was. Note, however, that the "very" test does not work with all adjectives – it typically works with the gradable adjectives, i.e. those we can think of in varying degrees, e.g. *quite/very/extremely inspired, inspiring, small, grateful*. On the other hand, we do not usually use adverbs such as *quite, slightly* or *very* to "grade" or modify adjectives such as *dead, complete, pregnant*, and *wonderful*. That's because something is, for example, either dead or it isn't; it cannot be somewhere in between. For this reason, many prescriptive grammarians object to expressions such as *very unique* because the adjective *unique* means "one of a kind", hence something cannot be more or less than one of a kind.

### Determiners

Imagine getting a message from a friend that reads *Bring book for class.* You wonder which book and which class she is referring to, so you ask her, and she clarifies that she means <u>*any*</u> *book* and <u>*tomorrow's*</u> *class.* The words *any* and *tomorrow's* help determine which book and which class she had in mind; hence they are called **determiners**, the next class of word we'll examine.

Determiners are words that come before a noun, and help to determine the reference of that noun. They belong to a broad class of words that includes articles such as the **definite article** *the* and the **indefinite articles** *a/an*, and the **demonstratives** *this*, *that*, *these* and *those*. Determiners may also include **possessive determiners** such as *my, her* and *Mary's*, **cardinal numbers** (i.e. numbers for counting) such as *seven*, **ordinal numbers** (i.e. numbers indicating order or sequence) such as *seventh*, **quantifiers** such as *some, many, few, several*, and other words such as *first* and *next*. Some determiners come as a combination of two or more words, such as *a lot of* and *some of*.

As you can see, these words all help us refer to more specifically to the noun that they precede, e.g. *that, Mary's, the last answer.*

Below is a table summarising the main types of determiners:

| Articles<br>Indefinite:<br>Definite: | *a, an*<br>*the* |
|---|---|
| Demonstratives<br>Singular:<br>Plural: | *this, that*<br>*these, those* |
| Possessive Determiners | *my, your, his, her, its, their* |
| Cardinal Numbers | *one, seven, fifty-eight, one thousand* |
| Ordinal Numbers | *seventh, fifty-eighth, one thousandth, last* |
| Quantifiers | *some, many, a few of, a lot of, several,*<br>*a couple of* |
| Other Determiners | *first, last, all, both, half, such* |

One key characteristic of determiners is that they do not stand alone, and must be followed by a noun. This distinguishes them from pronouns, which may stand alone because they take the place of nouns or noun phrases. Consider the following sentences:

20. *Those guitars are my instruments.*
21. *Those are mine.*

In 20, the words *those* and *my* are determiners as they precede nouns and do not stand alone. By contrast, in 21, *those* and *mine* stand alone (in fact, they mean "those guitars" and "my instruments" respectively), hence they are pronouns.

**Pronouns**

This brings us to **pronouns**. As we've already seen, pronouns stand in place of nouns, and this is seen in their name: the term *pronoun* comes from the Latin words *pro* (meaning "for" or "in place of") and *nomen* (meaning "name"). More accurately, however, pronouns stand not only in place of nouns, but also full noun phrases.

The most basic pronouns include the **personal pronouns** *I, me, you, she, her, he, him, it* and *they*. These are pronouns in that they stand in for whomever they happen to be referring to. We also have **possessive pronouns**, which indicate possession, such as *mine, yours, hers, his* and *theirs*; as we already saw in the sentence, <u>*Those*</u> *are* <u>*mine*</u>, when *mine* stands in for *my instruments*, it is a pronoun. Then there are **reflexive pronouns**, which end in *-self/selves*, namely *myself, yourself, himself, herself, itself* and *themselves*, and may stand on their own as they are pronouns, e.g. in *Help yourself.*

In addition, we also find pronouns at the start of relative clauses; these are called **relative pronouns** and take the form of *who, whom, that* and *which*, in noun phrases such as the following:

22. *the spy <u>who</u> loved me*
23. *the spy <u>whom</u> I loved*
24. *the file <u>that</u> contains all we know*
25. *the task <u>which</u> we were assigned*

We shall be taking a closer look at relative clauses in Chapter 3, but for now, let's just note that each relative pronoun (underlined in the noun phrases above) refers to a head noun: hence *who* and *whom* in the first two sentences refer to *spy*, *that* refers to *file* and *which* refers to *task*.

In addition to the above, there are many other words that function as pronouns even though they don't look like typical pronouns. Consider the following examples:

26. *I put tomato sauce on <u>everything</u>.*
27. *The <u>ones</u> with the new active ingredient are easily the best.*
28. *<u>These</u> are better than any that I've ever tried.*
29. *<u>Who(m)</u>/<u>what</u> do you prefer?*
30. *This is the <u>best</u>/<u>worst</u>/<u>least</u> we can expect.*

In 26, *everything* stands in for whatever the speaker happens to be referring to. Along with words such as *anything, anyone, someone, something* and *everyone*, it is an **indefinite pronoun** as it does not refer to any specific person or thing but whichever that happens to fit the description or context. In 27 and 28, the underlined are also pronouns as they stand in for the nouns that they happen to be referring to. Similarly, in 29, we have *who, whom* and *what*, which are called **interrogative pronouns** as they are pronouns that help us to ask questions, and in fact take the place of the entity that is being questioned (e.g. *you prefer <u>what</u>?*). Finally, in 30, we see that some words may function as pronouns if they stand in for noun phrases, e.g. *the best situation, the worst offer*.

The table below summarises the main types of pronouns:

| Personal Pronouns | *I, me, you, she, her, he, him, it, they* |
|---|---|
| Possessive Pronouns | *mine, yours, hers, his, its, theirs* |
| Reflexive Pronouns | *myself, yourself, himself, herself, itself, themselves* |
| Relative Pronouns | *who, whom, that, which* |
| Demonstrative Pronouns | *this, that, these, those* |
| Interrogative Pronouns | *who, whom, what* |
| Indefinite Pronouns | *any, some, anyone, anybody, anything, someone, somebody, something, everyone, everybody, whatever, whichever* |
| Other Pronouns | *best, worst, least, latest, newest* |

**Adverbs**

The term **adverb** literally means something that is added to verbs, so it should come as no surprise that their most typical function is to modify – or give us more information about – verbs. Adverbs typically tell us the time, manner, place, circumstances of and reasons for actions and processes, hence they answer "when", "how", "where", "why", and "with whom/what" questions.

The table below gives some examples of typical adverbs (underlined):

| *We must eat there <u>tomorrow</u>/<u>soon</u>/<u>often</u>.* | **Time/Frequency:** When? |
|---|---|
| *The calligrapher placed his pen <u>softly</u>/<u>carefully</u>/<u>gingerly</u> on the writing desk.* | **Manner:** How? |
| *The bus was parked <u>here</u>/<u>there</u>/<u>inside</u> this morning; The little car drove <u>past</u>/<u>on</u>/<u>away</u>/<u>off</u>.* | **Place:** Where? |

When people think of adverbs, they usually have in mind those that end in *-ly*, which are the adverbs of manner, and indeed, there are countless adverbs with this ending. However, do note that there are also a great many adjectives that end in *-ly*, such as *friendly*, *portly*, *early*, *surly* and *sickly*.

Apart from modifying verbs, adverbs also modify adjectives and adverbs, as the underlined adverbs in following examples show:

31. *Tom is <u>quite</u>/<u>very</u>/<u>extremely</u>/<u>frighteningly</u>/<u>less</u>/<u>more</u> intelligent.*
    (adverbs modifying the adjective, *intelligent*)

32. *Mariam speaks <u>rather</u>/<u>somewhat</u>/<u>very</u> fondly of her uncle.*
    (adverbs modifying the adverb, *fondly*)

In Chapter 5, we will be looking at something closely related to adverbs called adverbials – these may be single words or longer phrases that do the same job of adverbs. For example, using the sentences in the table above, we can also say *We must eat there next week* to tell the listener when we intend eating there, or *The little car drove straight on* to tell the listener the direction the car went. However, do bear in mind that the word "adverb" is a word-class label and should be applied to individual words only. In fact, *straight on* is made up of two adverbs, but in combination it is an adverbial.

### Grammar Detective

It is quite common to hear advice such as *Drive safe*. However, grammarians might point out that it is ungrammatical. Can you explain why this might be in terms of word class?

## Prepositions

Apart from nouns, verbs and adjectives, one of the most important class of words that a learner must master is **prepositions** – this is because they tell us about position and direction. They tell us where one noun is in relation to another noun (e.g. *The children are in school; the books on the shelf; government of the people*), or where an action is taking place in relation to a noun (e.g. *The mouse leapt towards the frightened cat; the cat ran under the table; the rat dived into the jar of cookies*).

The more typical prepositions include single words such as *in, at, on, under, beside, by, above* and *past*; however, some are made up of more than one word, such as *next to, on top of, apart from* and *in front of*. There are also prepositions that do not resemble any of these, yet do the job of prepositions, such as *including, regarding* and *according to*.

The most important thing to note about prepositions is that they always come before nouns or other grammatical constituents functioning as nouns: that's the reason they are called *pre*positions.

Many prepositions and adverbs share the same form, so it can often be difficult to tell them apart. However, if the word comes before a noun or some other constituent functioning as a noun, then it is a preposition, and if there is none following it, then it is an adverb. Take a look at the sentences below, both of which contain the word, *outside*:

33.  *We are often told we should think <u>outside</u> the box.*
34.  *When the weather is good, Mrs Lim prefers to sit <u>outside</u>.*

In the first sentence, *outside* is a preposition because it comes before a noun phrase and relates the action of thinking to the noun phrase, *the box*. By contrast, in the second sentence, the word *outside* tells us where Mrs Lim wishes to sit; hence, it is an adverb as it modifies a verb.

## Conjunctions

We'll now look at **conjunctions**, which are the last of the eight major word classes, and include words like *and, or, but, if, although* and *whether*. As their name implies, conjunctions are words that have the job of conjoining equivalent grammatical categories. These may be words of the same word class (e.g. noun + noun, adjective + adjective, verb + verb), and similar types of noun phrases or clauses or sentences.

In the following sentences, the underlined words are conjunctions:

35.  *My cat is small <u>but</u> fierce.*
36.  *Sheela loves playing the piano <u>and</u> violin.*
37.  *Jim will sell <u>or</u> rent a car.*

In sentence 35, *but* conjoins two adjectives, *small* and *fierce*, and signals a contrast (i.e. a small animal is not usually thought of as fierce). In 36, the conjunction *and* conjoins two nouns, *piano* and *violin*, and in 37, the conjunction *or* joins two verbs, *sell* and *rent*.

Conjunctions are also commonly found joining clauses and sentences, such as in the following sentences:

38.  *I'll visit you in London next year <u>if</u> I can take two weeks' leave.*
39.  *We will buy the apartment <u>when</u> prices are a little lower.*
40.  *Please let me know <u>before</u> you sign on the dotted line.*

In each of the sentences above, the conjunction joins two clauses – for example, in 39, the subordinating conjunction *when* joins two clauses: *we will buy the apartment* and *prices are a little lower.*

Some conjunctions are not single words, but come as pairs of words, for example *either ... or, neither ... nor,* and *not only ... but also.* These are known as *correlative conjunctions.* They also join equivalent grammatical categories, such as in the following sentence:

41.  *Ramesh was <u>neither</u> surprised <u>nor</u> thrilled to receive a call from his long-lost opponent.*

### Grammar Detective

Have a look at the following sentence:

*Joe is tired and going to bed now.*

Do you find the sentence odd or ungrammatical? If so, why?

## Other Word Classes

We've now finished examining the eight major word classes in English, but these are not all that can be found in the language: there are some other, minor word classes in English, some of them fairly common words.

The first of this is the infinitive "to". Have a look at the following sentence:

42.  *I'm going <u>to</u> cycle <u>to</u> school tomorrow.*

As you will have noticed, there are two instances of *to* above. The first one belongs to the verb *cycle*, while the second is a preposition as it precedes the noun *school*. Hence, they are different: the first *to* is called the infinitive "to" as it is a *to* that exists to form a *to*-infinitive, in this case *to cycle*. A *to*-infinitive is a verb in its simplest base form, without any endings that show tense or agreement. Hence, they are used as headwords in dictionaries.

Like the infinitive "to" above, another one-off use of a common word for a different purpose is the existential *there*, which is used solely to express the fact that something exists, e.g. <u>*There are seven people named John in my class*</u>. Note that this *there* tells us nothing about location, so it is different from the adverb *there*.

Interjections are another minor word class, and they include words such as *ah, ugh, argh, ouch* and *tsk*. In language varieties such as Singlish (or Colloquial Singapore English, to give its technical name), there are even discourse particles such as *lah, meh, ma* and *leh*.

## Analysing Word Class

Now that we've examined what word class is and what word classes English has, let's put this knowledge to practice.

As we've already seen, the word class of a word is determined not just by its meaning, but also its form (what it looks like) and its function (what it is doing in the phrase, clause or sentence).

Determining the word class of a word is often tricky as words of different word classes may share the same form, such as *there* and *to*, which we saw in the previous section. Hence, we shouldn't make snap judgements about word class; rather, we should always consider the meaning, form and function of each word. Let's try this with the sentence below:

43.  *When you have decided where to go during the holidays, contact
     my friend, who works as a travel agent and is able to give you
     good discounts.*

For each word, work out what word class it is, giving reasons for your
choice in the table. Fill in the table below – try to do this on your own
first, without checking the answers.

| Word | Word Class | Reason (Meaning, Form, Function) |
| --- | --- | --- |
| *when* | conjunction | It joins the clauses "you have decided … December holidays" and "contact my friend … a good discount". |
| *you* | pronoun | It refers to the person being spoken or written to. |
| *have* | verb | This is an auxiliary verb, and it shows present tense. |
| *decided* | verb | This is a main verb, which describes what the "you" is doing. |
| *where* | adverb | This is an interrogative adverb, which helps the speaker to enquire about the hearer's holiday destination. |
| *to* | infinitive "to" | It forms a *to*-infinitive with the following verb, i.e. "to go". |
| *go* | verb | It describes an action. |
| *during* | preposition | It precedes a noun phrase, "the holidays", and relates the action of "go" to it. |
| *the* | determiner | It comes before a noun, "holidays". |
| *holidays* | noun | It describes a concept (of a period when one does not have to go to work or school), and has an *-s* plural ending for plural nouns. |
| *contact* | verb | It describes what the speaker is asking the hearer to do. |

| | | |
|---|---|---|
| *my* | determiner | It comes before a noun, "friend", and helps the speaker determine which friend. |
| *friend* | noun | It is the name for a type of person. |
| *who* | pronoun | It is a relative pronoun, and refers to "friend". |
| *works* | verb | It describes an action. |
| *as* | preposition | It comes before a noun phrase, "a travel agent". |
| *a* | determiner | It comes before a noun, "(travel) agent". |
| *travel* | noun | It names an idea (the activity of travel). |
| *agent* | noun | It names a type of person. |
| *and* | conjunction | It joins two clauses, "who works as a travel agent" and "is able to give good discounts". |
| *is* | verb | It describes a state of being, and carries present tense. |
| *able* | adjective | It describes the travel agent. |
| *to* | infinitive 'to' | It forms a *to*-infinitive with the following verb, i.e. "to give". |
| *give* | verb | It describes an action. |
| *you* | pronoun | It refers to the hearer. |
| *good* | adjective | It describes the noun "discounts". |
| *discounts* | noun | It names a thing (discounts) and has a plural *-s* marker. |

## Conclusion

In this chapter, we investigated the eight major word classes in English, and some minor word classes. We also saw that the word class of a word depends not only on meaning, or form, but also on function. In subsequent chapters, we'll be looking at how words combine to form phrases, clauses, and ultimately, sentences.

# CHAPTER THREE

# NOUNS AND NOUN PHRASES

In Chapter 2, we looked at word classes. In this chapter, we will look at the different types of nouns and see how nouns may be combined with other words to form larger units known as noun phrases. We will explore ways to expand on individual nouns and move from simple descriptions of nouns via premodifications like articles and adjectives to more complex noun phrases that contain prepositional phrases or relative clauses.

We will see how nouns and heads of noun phrases are pertinent to grammar as they dictate whether we use singular or plural verbs in a sentence.

## NOUNS

Nouns are words that name people, places, things and ideas. They can be analysed as:

- Proper or common
- Concrete or abstract
- Countable or uncountable
- Collective nouns

The second distinction, concrete or abstract, has no effect on grammar, but the rest do – for example, in the use of determiners and the choice of singular and plural forms. Their effects will be discussed in this chapter.

## Proper vs Common

**Proper nouns** are (usually one-of-a-kind) names of specific people, places, organisations, occasions and festivals, months and years.

### How do we identify proper nouns?

- Proper nouns begin in a capital letter no matter where they appear in a sentence, like *Harry, Disneyland, Interpol, McDonald's, Deepavali* and *1971*.
- They do not normally take plurals. However, they <u>may</u> do so when a number is being specifically referred to: *There are two Eugenes and two Daniels in this class.*
- Typically, proper nouns do not take determiners, so *\*the Harry* and *\*a New York* are ungrammatical. (Note: the asterisk * is used to show ungrammaticality.) As with most rules of grammar, there are exceptions. For instance, in *the Hague* and *the United Kingdom*, the article "the" is part of the name of the place. There are also special uses such as *My dad is an Einstein* and *It's nothing like the Singapore I remember*. These special cases are allowed because *Einstein* and *Singapore* are not used as labels for unique references. When I say *It's nothing like the Singapore I remember*, I am thinking about and making comparisons between the Singapore I remember and the Singapore of today (more than one Singapore). Hence, *Singapore* is no longer a unique reference, and the use of the article "the" is allowed. In this regard, *Singapore* is used like a common noun.

**Common nouns,** on the other hand, are general labels for things, rather than specific ones. Some examples include *student, park, school, sleepover, celebration,* and *night.*

## Concrete vs Abstract

Nouns can be classified according to whether they have a physical form.

**Concrete nouns** refer to those that have a physical form and can be experienced through our senses, like our sense of touch or sight. Some examples include *kitten, teacher, telephone, cookie* and *handbag.*

**Abstract nouns** generally refer to ideas and concepts that do not have a physical form and thus cannot be seen, touched, tasted, heard or smelled, such as *pride, education, knowledge, success, love,* and *trust.* Many abstract nouns can be identified by their suffixes: *abili<u>ty</u>, content<u>ment</u>, sister<u>hood</u>, abrup<u>tness</u>,* and *gratifi<u>cation</u>.*

However, some nouns can be ambiguous: they have different senses that result in their being either concrete or abstract. Consider *light, morning* and *time.* Although we cannot physically touch light, see morning or time, there is no doubt that we can feel them or feel their effect on us. One could argue that you do not necessarily see *morning,* instead, what we identify with morning is the sun rising, the time of the day etc., making it an abstract noun. On the other hand, one might also argue that *light* could refer to something that contains a bulb and produces light – in which case it is a concrete noun. As for *time,* it may refer to a period during which one rests or work. In this instance, the *time* that is measured by hours and minutes is abstract. However, you could also ask someone for "the time" whereupon that person looks at his watch. *Time* is then more concrete: you actually look at something – your watch!

## Grammar Detective

Consider the following pairs of examples:

i.    *Art is an important component of culture.*
ii.   *My son's art is hanging in the living room.*

iii.  *I do not wish to sign up for that course because there*
      *will be a lot of homework.*
iv.   *I know it is overdue, but here is my homework.*

Are the underlined words abstract or concrete nouns?
Explain.

## Countable vs Uncountable

One of the most important distinctions between nouns is whether they
are countable or uncountable. This distinction affects grammar – whether
a singular or plural verb must follow the un/countable noun.

**Countable nouns** are those that can be counted, and have singular
and plural forms, for example, *one kitten, four kittens, two hundred kittens.*

## What are the properties of countable nouns?

- In English, countable nouns cannot stand alone in the singular
  form: *\*Boy is smart.* Singular countable nouns must always be
  used with determiners in a sentence: like an article (*a boy*), or a
  demonstrative (*that boy*), or a quantifier (*one boy*), or a possessive
  determiner (*her boy*).
- Plural countable nouns can be counted with quantifiers such
  as *few* and *many*, e.g. *few reasons, many reasons* (note that *little*

*reasons* and *much reasons* are ungrammatical, or non-standard). If we are making a comparison, we use the comparative quantifiers *fewer* and *more*, e.g. *fewer reasons, more reasons*. Note that *less reasons* and *lesser reasons* are regarded as non-standard although the former is very common among British, American and other speakers while the latter is common in Singapore.

### Regular vs Irregular Plurals

When a noun simply takes an *-s* to form the plural, it is said to have a regular plural form: *button –> buttons*. Nouns that end in a sibilant or hissing sound take *-es* to form the plural, for example, *kisses, brushes, quizzes*. Many nouns that end with a dental sound like "f" take *-ves*: *loaf –> loaves, knife –> knives*.

If a noun ends in a consonant (not "a, e, i, ou, u") plus *-y*, the usual plural form is *-ies* rather than *-ys*. Some examples include *baby –> babies, delivery –> deliveries*. If a noun ends with a vowel plus *-y* (such as *ay, ey*), then we simply add *-s* at the end of the noun to form the plural, e.g. *day –> days, monkey –> monkeys*. One thing to note is that proper nouns ending in *-y* usually are treated as if they were regular, e.g. *There are four Sandys in my class; I was born at a time when there were two Germanys*.

If a noun goes through some change other than those described above to form its plural, it is said to have an irregular plural form. Common examples include *woman –> women, ox –> oxen, foot –> feet, hypothesis –> hypotheses, curriculum –> curricula, syllabus –> syllabi*, and *formula –> formulae*. One may wonder why English has so many different ways of forming plurals. This is because historically, it has borrowed words from a number of languages. For instance, the word *ox* is of Germanic origin, *hypothesis* came from Greek, and *syllabus* and *formula* are from Latin. Some words like *syllabus* and *formula* have both regular and irregular plural forms. In mathematical and scientific contexts, the irregular plural form *mathematical formulae* is preferred, but in everyday senses, the regular plural is preferred, for example *formulas for happiness*. *Syllabi* is also considered more appropriate for academic purposes compared to the commonplace plural *syllabuses*.

Then there are other countable nouns that show no difference in the singular and plural forms: *a sheep / two sheep, a rare species / many species.*

**More on singular and plural noun forms:**
Some nouns may appear plural (possibly because they end with *-s*), but they are not: *news, physics, ethics* and *mathematics*. E.g. *This (piece of) <u>news</u> was made public yesterday.*

Some nouns can be both singular and plural, depending on their meaning. E.g. *<u>Statistics</u> is one of the compulsory courses students must read. These important <u>statistics</u> must be taken into consideration.*

Some nouns may appear singular in form, but they are plural in meaning: *public, police, youth. The police have arrested the burglars.*

### Grammar Detective

Can you think of the plural form for these nouns?

*salmon*
*aircraft*
*goose*
*mongoose*
*(computer) mouse*

Are you able to identify any discernible patterns to help you arrive at the correct plural forms? Use a dictionary if you are not sure.

**Uncountable nouns** refer to things that cannot be counted. These may include abstract ideas and concepts, as well as substances that cannot be divided into separate parts like *news, information, water, rice, bread, homework, equipment, furniture, luggage* and *knowledge*.

## What are the properties of uncountable nouns?

- Being uncountable, they generally do not have plural forms, so *four furnitures*, *three luggages* and *two homeworks* are regarded as incorrect. The non-standard plural forms are getting more common as more and more speakers use them. Surely you must have heard someone telling you how many *luggages* they came home with at the end of their trip. Many speakers of English use the uncountable nouns incorrectly, as seen in these pictures:

In fact, if you do a Google search for the word *softwares*, you will get approximately 42 million hits, and you will notice that the examples, as far as we can tell, come from a good mix of both native and non-native speakers of English.

- Since these nouns are uncountable, they are considered grammatically singular. This means that when they are the subject of a sentence, the verb that follows must take the singular form (as underlined) in *The furniture <u>looks</u> very classic* even if we happen to be talking about one bed, four chairs, two tables and three cupboards.

- If we need to 'count' uncountable nouns, we use words called *partitives* or *partitive nouns*, which are underlined in the following examples: *five <u>items</u> of shopping, two <u>bowls</u> of rice, three <u>spoonfuls</u> of sugar, three <u>pieces</u> of luggage, two <u>pieces</u> of software*. (Note that these partitives are countable nouns.)

- The determiners *much*, *little* and *less* are used with uncountable nouns. Thus, we say *much/little/less sugar* and not *\*many/\*few/ \*less sugars*.

Note that many nouns have both countable and uncountable uses, e.g. *I have no <u>idea</u> how he got there/I have no <u>ideas</u> for his birthday gift; There is not much <u>choice</u> around here/You have three <u>choices</u>*. Some nouns that are ordinarily uncountable may be used as countable nouns, e.g. *the finest teas, precious metals, simple sugars* – but this has the meaning of "specific varieties of tea/metal/sugar". Another example of this is the word *fruit* – it may be used as an uncountable noun, e.g. *I bought some* *fruit/three pieces of fruit*, but as a countable noun it has the meaning of "varieties of fruit", e.g. *This juice contains three tropical fruits: calamansi, banana* and *lemon*.

Consider the noun *money* – we can count how much we have in our wallets or purses, but grammatically speaking *money* is uncountable. So how do we explain that *money* is an uncountable noun?

Consider these points:

- There is no singular form of the word: *\*a money*. If you were to look up the word *money* in a dictionary, you may come across the plural form *monies*. However, this form is no longer used in Modern English, except in legal language.

- Think of the quantifier/s that you would pair with the word *money*: *I had little/\*few money left*. We ask someone *how much money they have*, and not *\*how many money they have*. Like other uncountable nouns, *money* is paired with *less/little/much/more* and not *few/many*.

- Like other uncountable nouns, *money* is grammatically singular and takes a singular verb: *Money isn't/\*aren't everything*.

Finally, note that most dictionaries label nouns as either C (countable) or U (uncountable). Something else to bear in mind is that some grammarians avoid both terms and instead refer to them as "count nouns" and "non-count nouns" because they believe there should be a distinction between nouns that describe things you can count physically and those that the language treats as countable or uncountable.

## Collective Nouns

Traditionally, when we consider the term "collective noun", we think of examples like these – *a gaggle of geese, a band of musicians, a troupe of dancers, a flutter of butterflies and a pack of hounds.*

Here are some collective nouns referring to birds which you may find interesting:

| | | |
|---|---|---|
| *a peep of chickens* | *a murder of crows* | *a parliament of owls* |
| *a paddling of ducks* | *a charm of finches* | *an unkindness of ravens* |

These are useful for the teaching of vocabulary but are of little relevance to grammar, so we will not be looking at these types of collective nouns.

The **collective nouns** (also sometimes referred to as **group nouns**) that we will discuss in this section include words that refer to groups of people or animals as a unit or a set: the members can decide whether to act together as one or as separate individuals. Some examples include *group, team, staff, audience, committee, army, class, government, crew, choir,* and *family.*

When you look up a word like *team* in an advanced learner's dictionary, you will find that it is paired with both singular and plural verbs. Why is this the case? In British English, collective nouns can take either singular verbs or plural verbs. The singular verb is preferred when the members are acting in unison as a single unit, whereas the plural verb is used when the members are acting as individuals who just happen to be part of the group:

1. *The class has agreed to make a trip to the museum.*
   (acting as one group = singular verb)

2. *The class have been arguing about the year-end project.*
   (acting as separate individuals = plural verb)

In British English, the singular words for groups of people like that in the second example are often used with plural verbs and plural pronouns, e.g. *My staff are upset with me because they feel I have let them down.* However it is uncommon for singular collective nouns to take plural verbs in American English. Singapore English generally follows American usage in this respect, although in sports reporting, team names are used with plural verbs, as is the norm in British English, e.g. *Singapore were surprisingly strong in the SEA Games; Chelsea are finally playing as they should.* In British English, it is also common to use plural verbs with organisations and businesses, e.g. *London Transport are hiring new staff.*

Many speakers and students of English consider uncountable nouns like *furniture* and *software* collective nouns because these words refer to a "collection" or group of items. Collective nouns like *committee* and *government* are different; they can be used in the plural sense, for example *committees, governments, classes* while uncountable nouns do not take the plural *-s* form (*\*furnitures, \*softwares*).

### Grammar Detective

Read the following text. Pick out all the nouns you can find, and label each one accordingly:

proper or common
concrete or abstract

Are there any you are not completely sure about? Why?

*A family were frightened out of their home by large spiders last Saturday. Madam Lee and her two sons have moved out of their house. She said the spiders were seen in her kitchen when renovation works were being carried out. "We identified the species of the spider using the internet," she shared. According to spider enthusiasts, the Bushy-footed Trapdoor spider is rarely sighted in Singapore.*

## Grammar Detective

Can you spot any errors in the sentences below? If so, which word or words would you change? Can you explain the errors in terms of what you know about nouns?

i.    The check-in officer advised Jennifer not to check in more than two luggages.

ii.   Mr Donovan found his students' feedbacks very useful.

iii.  The teacher's advice were what he needed.

iv.   I returned from my vacation and found 203 e-mails in my inbox!

v.    I'll have three coffees and two chocolate muffins, please.

vi.   The police does not have the latest information on the accident.

vii.  The committee has had serious disagreements over the collective sale.

viii. The deers attract many visitors to the park.

ix.   Our table tennis team have done us proud at the Olympics.

x.    The clothings she gave away were still in good condition.

## NOUN PHRASES

In this section we will look closely at **noun phrases**. A phrase is made up of a group of words that contains a head word which tells you what the phrase is about, and also other words which modify or add more information to the head. The head of a noun phrase is a noun. Let's take the noun *teachers* as an example. One could add more information to describe the type of teachers referred to, like this:

| Noun Phrase | | | |
|---|---|---|---|
| determiner | adjective | noun | head noun |
| *the* | *busy* | *science* | *teachers* |

You could further narrow down the possible referents to the noun *teachers* by adding words after the **head noun**:

| Noun Phrase | | | | |
|---|---|---|---|---|
| determiner | adjective | noun | head noun | relative clause |
| *the* | *busy* | *science* | *teachers* | *who like to dress in black and punish students who give incorrect answers* |

Words that provide more information on the head noun are called modifiers. **Premodifiers** which appear before the head noun may consist of determiners, adjectives and nouns. **Postmodifiers**, on the other hand, may consist of prepositional phrases, relative clauses, non-finite clauses, postpositive adjectives and adverbs.

So, noun phrases are structured as:

| Premodifier | | Postmodifier |
|---|---|---|
| **(i) Determiners**<br>• Articles<br>  *a, an, the*<br>• Demonstratives<br>  *this, that, these, those*<br>• Quantifiers<br>  *some, two, fifth*<br>• Possessives<br>  *our, her, Marianne's*<br><br>**(ii) Adjectives**<br>*strange, beautiful, unpredictable*<br><br>**(iii) Nouns**<br>*insect, plant, animal* | **+** **Head Noun** *world* **+** | **(i) Prepositional phrases**<br>*without borders*<br><br>**(ii) Relative Clauses**<br>*which is rapidly changing*<br><br>**(iii) Non-Finite Clauses**<br>*ruled by the internet*<br><br>**(iv) Postpositive Adjectives**<br>*united*<br><br>**(v) Adverbs**<br>*beyond* |

## Premodifiers

### Determiners

There are three kinds of determiners: **predeterminers**, **central determiners**, and **postdeterminers**. As the following table shows, there is a strict order that these should follow:

| Determiners | | | Head Noun |
|---|---|---|---|
| **Predeterminers**<br>*all, both, half, one-third, such* | **Central Determiners**<br>*the, a/an, each, every, some, any* | **Postdeterminers**<br>*first, last, many, a lot of, several, eight* | *students* |

Note that there can be only one predeterminer or central determiner in a noun phrase, but there can usually be more than one postdeterminer, e.g. *all the last eight students.*

## Adjectives

Let's take a closer look at adjectives. Adjectives that describe a noun may appear either within a noun phrase or outside it or after a linking verb.

When the adjective appears inside a noun phrase, it is used as:

- an **attributive adjective** that premodifies a noun, e.g. *a scorned woman*
- a **postpositive adjective** that postmodifies a noun, e.g. *a woman scorned*

When the adjective appears outside a noun phrase, after a linking verb, it is known as:

- the **predicative adjective**, e.g. *(The woman) is scorned*.

Did you know that you have to include hyphens when you use a compound adjective attributively before the head noun it describes? For instance, you say *The four-year-old girl was found missing* where the compound adjective is hyphenated.

When the same expression is used predicatively after a linking verb like *was*, there is no need for hyphens: *She was four years old.*

When the compound adjective involves measurement, it is singular in form when it is used attributively (*the fifteen-centimeter-long ruler*), but plural when it is used predicatively (*The ruler is fifteen centimeters long.*)

There is an exception to the hyphenation rule: if the head adjective is modified by an *-ly* adverb, it is not hyphenated even if used attributively, e.g. *her newly acquired handbag*. This is an exception and there is no grammatical basis for it.

When more than one adjective is used attributively, they usually follow a certain sequence: opinion/value > size > age/temperature > shape > colour > origin > material. Some examples are:

| opinion/value | *beautiful* | *expensive* |
|---|---|---|
| size | *small* | |
| age/temperature | *old* | |
| shape | | *oblong* |
| colour | *beige* | *brown* |
| origin | *Italian* | *Korean* |
| *material | *metallic* | *wooden* |

For example, when you combine a determiner like *a* to multiple adjectives to describe a head noun like *bag*, you get: *a beautiful small old beige Italian metallic bag*, and not *\*a small old beautiful beige metallic Italian bag*. In the table above, note the asterisk (\*) in front of "material". In noun phrases like *a metal box* and *my silver bracelet*, the words referring to the materials the box and bracelet are made of are not adjectives. If you were to look up these words in a dictionary, you will find that they are labelled as nouns. The adjectival forms of *metal* and *silver* are "metallic" and "silvery". However, if the word *silver* refers to the colour of the bracelet (not the material or substance it is made from), then it is an adjective (of colour).

Many terms denoting nationality or ethnicity have identical adjective and noun forms. For example, the words of nationality or ethnicity like *Singaporean, Malay, Indian, Chinese, Japanese, French, Burmese, American, Swiss, Italian, Thai* can be used as an adjective:

3.  *his Singaporean wife* (a premodifying adjective)
4.  *His wife is (very) Singaporean.* (premodified by the adverb, *very*)

Or a noun:

5.    *His wife is <u>a</u> Singaporean.* (preceded by a determiner like *a*)
6.    *They are <u>amazing</u> Singaporeans.* (takes the adjective premodifier, *amazing*, and the plural *-s* suffix)

### Grammar Detective

Consider these two sentences:

i.     *I love eating ice cream made from strawberries.*
ii.    *I love eating strawberry ice cream.*

What is the word class of the word *strawberries/strawberry* in both sentences – are they adjectives or nouns? State your reasons. Use a dictionary if you are not sure.

### Grammar Detective

In traditional grammar, any word that premodifies a noun was considered an adjective. However, we now make a distinction between the different types of premodifiers. Look back at the structure of noun phrases on page 59. Now consider the underlined words in the noun phrases below. Decide if they are nouns or adjectives. (Clue: One way to test for nouns is to combine the word with only a determiner.)

i.     the <u>poster</u>
ii.    the <u>campus</u> poster
iii.   the <u>campus rally</u> poster
iv.    the <u>campus rally committee</u> poster
v.     the <u>big</u> poster
vi.    the <u>incredible</u> campus

Were you able to tell the difference?

## Compound Nouns

When we have noun + head noun combinations, which are also known as **compound nouns**, we can often swap the words around and insert a preposition in between the two words:

> *ice cube* = cube (of) ice
> *bird cage* = cage for bird(s)
> *dancing shoes* = shoes for dancing

If the noun premodifier is a material/substance, we can usually add "made of": *copper kettle* = *kettle <u>made of</u> copper*; *gold pen* = *pen <u>made of</u> gold* (only if *gold* means the material, not just the colour). Note that traditionally, compound nouns referred only to single words that were formed by combining two nouns, like *toothpaste, hairbrush, football* and *blackboard*.

### Grammar Detective

Where can we find compound nouns? Look at food labels and newspaper headlines. Here are some examples.

Another point to think about is the order of the nouns. Does it matter which noun comes first in the sequence of noun + noun? Is meaning affected by the sequence? Consider these two pairs of compound nouns:

*flower garden* vs *garden flower*
*chocolate milk* vs *milk chocolate*

There is often a fine line between premodifying adjectives and nouns. Consider these examples: *gold pen, wool sweater* and *Chinese silk.* If *gold* describes the colour of the pen, it is an adjective. (Colour words are generally used as adjectives, and they precede the noun that they modify.) However, if the pen is made of gold, then *gold* is a noun premodifier (referring to the material). In the noun phrase *wool sweater, wool* is a noun that refers to the soft, fine hair that covers animals like sheep.

*Wool* premodifies the head noun *sweater*. The word has an adjective form: *woollen*. Words like *Chinese* that refer to the place of origin is an adjective: we can rephrase this predicatively to say, *The silk is Chinese*.

## Postmodifiers

In the table on page 59, we saw that there are five types of postmodifiers: prepositional phrases, relative clauses, non-finite clauses, postpositive adjectives and postpositive adverbs. How do we determine what type of postmodifier we see in a noun phrase? The answer lies in the *first word* following the head noun.

### Prepositional Phrases

If the first word in the postmodifier is a preposition, then the postmodifier is a **prepositional phrase**. Examples of noun phrases with a prepositional phrase as a postmodifier include:

7.  *cars <u>with low suspension</u>*
8.  *parcels <u>for every student</u>*
9.  *your book <u>on the table</u>*

### Relative Clauses

When the postmodifier begins with *who, whom, what, which* or *that*, it is a **relative clause**. These are called relative pronouns because they relate to the head noun immediately preceding them:

10. *the author <u>who refuses to sign his books</u>*
11. *the book <u>that I bought recently</u>*

Relative clauses contain a verb and all the participants that the verb requires (e.g. subject, object). (Do not worry about clauses for now as we will examine them later in Chapter 5.) Relative pronouns stand in for or refer to the head noun they follow, so in *the book <u>that</u> I bought recently*, the relative pronoun *that* refers to *book*.

In English, the relative pronoun may be omitted if it is the object of the relative clause but not if it is the subject. Hence, it is alright to say *She found the book (that) I bought recently*, where *that* refers to the object of the verb *bought* in the relative clause and could be omitted. However, in the example, *She found the book that costs $30,* the subject pronoun *that* cannot be omitted: *\*She found the book costs $30* is ungrammatical.

Note that there are some relative clauses that begin in words like *when* and *where*, if they refer to time and place: *the day when the accident occurred, the party where we first met*. Although *when* and *where* are not relative pronouns (they are relative adverbs), it is helpful to analyse the clauses *when the accident happened* and *where we first met* as relative clauses.

There are two types of relative clauses in English: restrictive and non-restrictive. **Restrictive** (identifying/defining) **relative clauses** (or noun phrases) refer to *only* a particular group; statement is *restricted* to this group. **Non-restrictive** (non-identifying/non-defining) **relative clauses** (or noun phrases) merely add optional information.

Restrictive relative clauses or noun phrases are not set off with commas:

12. *The handbag that/which she carried yesterday was new.*
13. *Students who behave rowdily should be sent for counselling regularly.*

In sentence 12, the writer is identifying the handbag by stating that it is the one she carried yesterday, as opposed to any other handbags she might already own. In sentence 13, the writer identifies which students should be sent for counselling regularly by restricting it to those who behave rowdily.

Non-restrictive relative clauses or noun phrases are set off with commas:

14. *The handbag, which she carried yesterday, was made of leather and cost a fortune.*
15. *Students, who behave rowdily, should be sent for counselling regularly.*

In sentence 14 above, there is no need to identify the handbag because it is already mentioned. Here the writer merely provides a bit of background context by telling the readers that she carried the handbag yesterday. Commas indicate something that is a given, and so the non-restrictive relative clauses merely provide additional information, not restrict information. In sentence 15, the writer seems to suggest students should be sent for counselling regularly because students (all of them!) behave rowdily.

**Grammar Detective**

Is there a difference in meaning between the first and second sentences in each pair below?

i.    *My sister who is abroad has sent me a postcard.*
ii.   *My sister, who is abroad, has sent me a postcard.*

iii.  *Snakes which are venomous should be avoided.*
iv.   *Snakes, which are venomous, should be avoided.*

**Non-finite Clauses**

When the first word of the postmodifier is a non-finite verb, i.e. a verb that does not show tense, the postmodifier is a **non-finite clause**. The underlined words in the following noun phrases are non-finite verbs:

16. *cookies <u>shared</u> at the pantry*
17. *letters <u>written</u> by angry parents*
18. *families <u>attending</u> the funfair*

The verb forms *shared*, *written* and *attending* with the *-d*, *-en* and *-ing* participles do not carry tense. We will examine these later in the next chapter. Sometimes the non-finite clause postmodifier is not so easy to spot. In the noun phrase *the writer widely criticised for his extreme views on politics*, the first word in the postmodifier is the adverb *widely*, but the main word in the clause is still the verb *criticised*, which the adverb modifies.

## Postpositive Adjectives
A postmodifier is a **postpositive adjective** if the word following the head noun is an adjective. There aren't many postpositive adjectives in English, but some common examples include *a country divided/united*, *a woman scorned*, *heir apparent* and *proof positive*. Typically, postpositive adjectives are used with indefinite pronouns, i.e. pronouns that do not refer to specific things or people: *someone special*, *something useful*, and *anything available*.

## Postpositive Adverbs
In the noun phrase *a world beyond,* the adverb *beyond* appears immediately after the head noun *world*. Typically, postpositive adverbs indicate place and may be modified by prepositions or other adverbs, as seen in *over <u>there</u>, right <u>here</u>.*

## Head Nouns
In the example *families attending the funfair,* which we saw earlier, the noun phrase is made up of the noun *families* plus the non-finite clause postmodifier *attending the funfair*. The noun *families* is referred

to as the **head noun**, which is also the most important word in the noun phrase.

To find the head noun of a noun phrase, look out for nouns and see which are followed by typical postmodifiers like prepositional phrases and relative clauses. In English, verbs agree with subjects, and when the subject is a noun phrase containing several nouns, the verb normally agrees with the head noun:

19. *The <u>poster</u> for the campaign <u>is</u> effective.*
20. *The <u>posters</u> for the campaign <u>are</u> effective.*

From the examples above, it can be seen that the verbs agree with *poster* and *posters* and not the other noun in the subject position, *campaign.* So the head noun is *poster/posters.*

If you look at any text, you will be able to find quite a few noun phrases. Sometimes it may be hard to spot a noun phrase immediately or to determine where a noun phrase begins and ends. Here are some ways to spot a noun phrase:

- Ask a **who/what question**: Who/what are pronouns. The answer to this question should elicit the noun phrase.
- **Pronoun replacement**: Try replacing the noun phrase with an appropriate pronoun. Pronouns replace entire noun phrases, not parts of noun phrases.
- See if the noun phrase you have identified is a **constituent**: phrases are constituents, or independent, meaningful, standalone units.

Let's consider this sentence:

21. *The boy with a weird name often bakes cupcakes with chocolate frosting for fun.*

When we apply the who/what question test, we will identify the following noun phrases:

Who? *The boy with a weird name*
What? *cupcakes with chocolate frosting*

When we apply the pronoun replacement test, we can see that *The boy with the weird name* can be substituted with the pronoun *he:*

*He often bakes cupcakes with chocolate frosting for fun.*
but NOT
*\*He with a weird name often bakes cupcakes with chocolate frosting for fun.*

Similarly, we can substitute the noun phrase *cupcakes with chocolate frosting* with the pronoun *them.*

When we use the constituent test, we find that a meaningful unit would seem to be:

*The boy with a weird name*
but NOT
*\*The boy with a weird name often*

Another point to note is sometimes noun phrases may be embedded in larger noun phrases. If you look closely at the noun phrase *cupcakes with chocolate frosting*, there is another noun phrase embedded it – *chocolate frosting*. This embedded noun phrase can also be substituted with the question word "what" and the pronoun "it".

## Grammar Detective

There are many noun phrases in the extract below. Identify all the noun phrases and analyse their structure by identifying the head noun, and type of premodifier and postmodifier you can find.

*Dolphins are social, living in pods of up to a dozen individuals. In places with a high abundance of food, pods can join temporarily, forming an aggregation called a superpod; such groupings may exceed a thousand dolphins. The individuals communicate using a variety of clicks, whistles and other vocalizations. They also use ultrasonic sounds for echolocation. Membership in pods is not rigid; interchange is common. However, the cetaceans can establish strong bonds between each other. This leads to them staying with injured or ill individuals, even actively helping them to breathe by bringing them to the surface if needed. This altruistic behaviour does not appear to be limited to their own species, however. A dolphin in New Zealand that goes by the name of Moko has been observed to seemingly help guide a female Pygmy Sperm Whale together with her calf out of shallow water.*

*Source: http://aiweb.cs.washington.edu/research/projects/ai6/xiaoling/random_wiki_pages/Dolphin*

## Pronouns

There are different types of pronouns in English:

- **Personal pronouns** are means of identifying speakers, addressees, and others:
  *I, we, he, she, you, it, they, me, us, him, her*

- **Possessive pronouns** express ownership:
  *mine, ours, his, hers, theirs, yours*
  Note: these are different from possessive determiners which cannot stand alone: <u>*my*</u> *car,* <u>*our*</u> *books,* <u>*your*</u> *bag*

- **Reflexive pronouns** always end in *-self* or *-selves*, referring to a noun (phrase) or pronoun that appears elsewhere in the clause:
  *myself, ourselves, yourself, yourselves, himself, herself, itself, themselves, oneself*

- **Reciprocal pronouns** express a two-way relationship:
  *each other, one another*

- **Demonstrative pronouns** show contrast between "near" and "distant":
  *this, that, these, those*
  Note: *this*, for instance, can be used as a pronoun (<u>*This*</u> *is yours*) or as a demonstrative determiner (<u>*This*</u> *book is yours.*)

- **Indefinite pronouns** express a less specific meaning:
  *someone, something, somebody, anyone, anybody, anything, everyone, everybody*

- **Relative pronouns** are used to link a relative clause:
  *who, whom, whose, which, that* used in a relative clause like:
  *(the book)* <u>*that*</u> *you borrowed yesterday*

- **Interrogative pronouns** are used to ask questions about other nouns:

  *who, whom, whose, which, what* used in a question like:

  <u>*Which*</u> *is mine?*

  Note: these are different from interrogative determiners:

  <u>*Which*</u> *book is mine?*

Reciprocal pronouns, *each other* and *one another,* are used to refer to actions that two people are doing at the same time. Many speakers of English use the two pronouns interchangeably i.e. they share the same meaning. Some grammarians claim that *each other* is more common in speech than *one other;* hence, more informal. Others believe that *each other* is more suitable to refer to the relationship between two individuals while *one another* is used to focus on groups of people or things.

## First, Second or Third?

The system of naming first, second and third persons is based on the distance from the speaker. For instance, *I* refers to the speaker, *you* to the listener which could be singular or plural, and *he/she/they* to some other party, removed from the speaker.

- **First person pronoun**:

  *I/me/myself/mine* (singular); *we/us/ourselves/ours* (plural)

- **Second person pronoun**:

  *you/yourself/yours* (both singular and plural)

- **Third person pronoun**:
  *he/him/himself/his; she/her/herself/hers, it/itself/its* (singular);
  *they/them/themselves/theirs* (plural)

### Subject vs Object Pronoun

Pronouns of English are sensitive to the position in which they appear in a sentence. They can take a subject or an object position:

|      | Subject | Verb | Object |
|------|---------|------|--------|
| 22a. | *The doctor who acts part-time* | *knows* | *my sister.* |
| 22b. | *He* | *knows* | *her.* |
| 22c. | *\*Him* | *knows* | *she.* |

The last example is ungrammatical because a **subject pronoun** should appear in subject position, but *him* is an object pronoun. Other examples include *I, we, he, she, they*. Also, an **object pronoun** should appear in object position, but *she* is a subject pronoun. Other object pronouns include *me, us, him, her, them*.

Combining the terminology, we refer to *he* as a third-person singular subject pronoun, and *her* as a third-person singular object pronoun.

### More on Object Pronouns

Another point to note is that, after a preposition, the pronoun is always in the object form, for example *for/to/with/about/towards/of me* (not *\*I*). Consider this pair of examples:

*My team and I will give our best to this community.*

*\*This is an important opportunity for my team and I to show our abilities.*

The second example is ungrammatical because after the pronoun *for*, the object pronouns are required: *for my team and <u>me</u>*, or *for <u>us</u>*.

The same rule applies to interrogative pronouns *who* and *whom*: *who* is a subject pronoun, whereas *whom* is an object pronoun which appears in the object position as well as after prepositions. When in doubt, try substituting the interrogative pronouns with a subject pronoun like *he/she/they* or an object pronoun like *him/her/them*.

### *Grammar Detective*

Consider the pronouns in these examples. Which sentence is correct? State your reasons.

i.    *He is faster than me.*
ii.   *He is faster than I am.*
iii.  *He is faster than I.*

## Pronominal Reference

Let us look at **pronominal reference**, that is, how pronouns refer to the nouns, noun phrases and noun-like constituents they stand in for – in other words, their *referents*. When a pronoun refers backwards in a sentence or text to its referent, this is known as **anaphoric reference**:

23.  *She is afraid of <u>all types of bugs</u>. <u>They</u> scare her.*

←

Note that *they* comes after its referent, *all types of bugs*.

When a pronoun refers forwards to find its referent, i.e. the pronoun appears before the referent, then this is **cataphoric reference:**

24.  *She* is an amazingly generous person. *My mom* is my role model.
     →

Finally, when a pronoun refers to something that is not mentioned in the text, this is called **exophoric reference**. Imagine a scenario where a mother steps into her teenage son's room and upon seeing a mess, she exclaims: *I want you to clear this now!* We know that the demonstrative pronoun *this*, which does not have a referent in the text (either spoken or written), refers to the mess she sees. The mother does not have to use the word *mess* before being able to use the pronoun *this* as the meaning is very clear from the context.

He was eating dinner when the phone rang.

subject + was / were + verb + ing

7pm - 7:20pm

7:15pm

# CHAPTER FOUR

# VERBS AND VERB PHRASES

Have you noticed how it is almost impossible to construct sentences without verbs? That's because verbs are central to clauses, the building blocks of sentences.

In this chapter, we will focus on verbs and verb phrases. We will begin by looking at some basic points about verbs before moving on to analysing verb phrases.

## VERBS

There are a few ways of classifying verbs:
- Main/lexical or auxiliary
- Meaning
- Stative or dynamic
- Verb forms
- Finite or non-finite
- Intransitive, transitive, etc. (discussed in Chapter 5)

## Main/Lexical vs Auxiliary Verbs

The first classification groups verbs as either **main/lexical** verbs or **auxiliary** verbs. Main verbs carry the meaning of the action or process. Auxiliary verbs, on the other hand, carry other types of information – tense, aspect and modality. There are two types of auxiliary verbs – primary and modal auxiliaries – which will be discussed later in this chapter.

Consider the following sentences. The verbs are labelled as main (m) or auxiliary (a):

1.  *The mouse <u>could</u> <u>have</u> <u>been</u> <u>hiding</u> in the jar.*
        a       a       a         m

2.  *You <u>should</u> really <u>think</u> about this carefully.*
         a                m

3.  *I <u>am</u> <u>reading</u> as fast as I can.*
        a      m

4.  *That poor child <u>is</u> asleep.*
                          m

## Verb Meaning

Using the functional approach to grammar, verbs can be classified based on their meaning:

- **Action verbs** describe processes of "doing" which require physical action. Action verbs include *hit, jump, sing, perform, write* and *bite.* The actions could be intentional like *running,* or unintentional like *fell.* They may also refer to abstract doings and happenings, for example, *He <u>failed</u> to qualify for the competition.* In other instances, the doer may not be endowed with human consciousness, as seen in *The leaves <u>rustled</u> in the breeze.*

- **Linking** or **copular verbs** link nouns to a description, and they act like "=" signs. This is typically expressed by the verb *to be (is, are, was,* etc.*)* which links a thing and its attribute, as seen in: *The students <u>are</u>/<u>grew</u>/<u>became</u>/<u>felt</u>/<u>seemed</u>/<u>looked</u> tired.* These verbs are also used to identify things like *The prettiest girl in my class <u>was</u>/<u>became</u> the winner of Miss Singapore last year.*

- **Saying verbs** are used for speech or talking: *Jamie <u>said</u>/<u>screamed</u>/<u>shouted</u>/<u>claimed</u> that she was in a lot of pain.*

- **Sensing verbs** (also called verbs of perception) are verbs that are related to the five senses: *see, hear, taste, smell, feel.* An example of a sensing verb in a sentence is *Mandy could <u>hear</u> her mother calling out her name.*

- **Existential verbs** help say a person or thing exists. English uses the construction *there is/are/was/have been/*etc. as seen in *There <u>are</u>/<u>live</u> two angry birds in that house.*

- **Mental verbs** have to do with thinking and knowing. Some examples include *think, know, need, want, suspect, imagine, feel, believe* as in *Only Peter <u>knows</u> Spiderman's true identity.*

Verbs can sometimes be used in more than one way. Consider the verbs feel and smell, and think of the different ways we can use those verbs.

*Sandy <u>felt</u> hungry.*                                          linking
                                                          ("Sandy" = "hungry")
*Sandy <u>felt</u> something crawl up her back.*         sensing

> *Sandy felt sorry for the little boy.*          mental
> *Sandy felt the table surface.*                 action
>
> *The puppy smelled bad.*                         linking
> *The puppy smelled Johnny's dirty socks.*        action

## Stative vs Dynamic

Another classification for verbs separates them into either stative or dynamic. **Stative** verbs like *know*, *understand*, *like*, and *love* describe *states*, which are not observable and typically have no clear start or end point. Because of these reasons, stative verbs are generally not used in the progressive/continuous aspect:

5.  I *understand*/*know* how you must feel.
6.  *I *am understanding*/*knowing* how you must feel.

However, in certain occasions, it is possible to use the stative verb in the progressive *-ing* form to mean "at this very moment": *I felt fine this morning, but I am having a terrible headache now.* In general, stative verbs refer to the following:

- thoughts: *believe, remember, understand, want,*
- likes and dislikes: *dislike, hate, love, prefer*
- possession: *have, own, possess, contain*
- senses: *look, seem, sound, taste*

**Dynamic** verbs typically describe actions which are observable: *run, skip, swim, cut,* and *drive*. These verbs can take the *-ing* form:

7.  The little girl *is skipping* to class.
8.  The kids *are swimming* in the pool.

Consider this utterance:

*Try this milk. It is smelling funny to me.*

Does the sentence sound funny or weird to you? Does it have to do with the way the verb *smell* is used? Perhaps it is better to phrase the second sentence in this manner: *It smells funny to me.* When *smell* is used as a stative verb, it is odd to use it in the *-ing* form. Consider this pair of examples:

*This coffee tastes really bitter.*
*The baker is tasting the pie.*

*Taste* is a verb like *smell*. What the examples above show is that *taste* can be used as both a stative verb in the first sentence and a dynamic verb in the second.

## Verb Forms

Let's now consider another way of classifying verbs – based on their forms. Verbs can take the following forms:

- **base form**:      *approve*     *take*     *put*
- **-s present tense**:    *approves*    *takes*    *puts*
- **-ing participle**:    *approving*   *taking*   *putting*
- **-ed past tense**:    *approved*    *took*    *put*
- **-ed/en participle**:   *approved*    *taken*    *put*

You will note that verbs like *approve* are regular verbs because their forms follow exactly the labels in bold on the left. As for *take* and *put*, we find that they take irregular forms because the past tense of *take* is *took*, while the past tense and participle forms of the verb *put* is also *put*.

Now let's take a closer look at each verb form. The **base form** is the most basic form of a verb, with no inflections or suffixes. It is also the form that is listed in the dictionary. Some examples are:

9.   *They <u>buy</u> me presents every birthday.*
10.  *She will <u>go</u> to school tomorrow.*

The **-s present tense** form is used only with third person singular subjects:

11.  *My sister <u>likes</u> Ben and Jerry's ice cream.*
12.  *The English teacher who <u>likes</u> ice cream <u>is</u> my sister.*

Next, we consider verbs with the **-ing participle**. Note that some words ending with *-ing* are not necessarily verbs; they are sometimes used as adjectives: *This is an <u>interesting</u> movie; She is really <u>irritating</u>*. Verbs with the *-ing* participle sometimes pose a different challenge to less proficient students – spelling. Very often, *-ing* verbs involve a spelling change like:

13.  *visit → visiting*
14.  *beg → begging*
15.  *panic → panicking*
16.  *create → creating*

The **-ed past tense** form is used to show past tense. As we have seen earlier, some verbs have irregular past tense forms:

17.  *Susan's mother <u>baked</u> her a chocolate cake last weekend.* (regular)
18.  *Susan <u>ran</u> in yesterday's race.* (irregular)

Finally, we look at the ***-ed/en* participle**, so called because some verbs take *-ed* while others take *-en*:

19. *<u>Captivated</u> by her beauty, the prince fell in love with Cinderella.*
20. *The hungry worker has <u>eaten</u> a chicken sandwich, a chocolate bar, and a slice of cake.*

## Finite vs Non-finite Verbs

An important grammatical distinction between verbs is whether they are finite or non-finite. Finite verbs show contrasts in the following: tense, number and person.

On the other hand, non-finite verbs do not show any such contrasts and do not change their form. Look at the following chart, which lists the different types of finite and non-finite verbs. Note that only the verbs in bold are finite/non-finite.

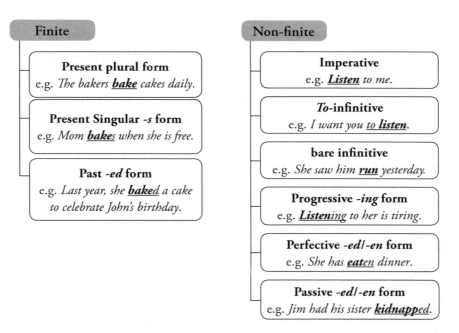

**Finite**

**Present plural form**
e.g. *The bakers **bake** cakes daily.*

**Present Singular *-s* form**
e.g. *Mom **bake**s when she is free.*

**Past *-ed* form**
e.g. *Last year, she **bake**d a cake to celebrate John's birthday.*

**Non-finite**

**Imperative**
e.g. ***Listen** to me.*

***To*-infinitive**
e.g. *I want you to **listen**.*

**bare infinitive**
e.g. *She saw him **run** yesterday.*

**Progressive *-ing* form**
e.g. ***Listen**ing to her is tiring.*

**Perfective *-ed/ -en* form**
e.g. *She has **eaten** dinner.*

**Passive *-ed/ -en* form**
e.g. *Jim had his sister **kidnapp**ed.*

**Finite Verbs**

There are two tenses in English: present and past. English does not have a true future tense as there are no special markings on verbs to indicate the future. Instead, we use modals, for example, *I shall/will write tomorrow after a good night's sleep.* The modal verb *shall/will* is used to talk about a future event, unlike the *-ed* suffix which is used to show past tense.

In the following examples, the verbs are **finite** because they show contrast in **tense** (past or present):

| | | |
|---|---|---|
| 21a. | *Siti <u>sings</u> all the time.* | present |
| 21b. | *Sit <u>sang</u> at the concert last month.* | past |

Next, finite verbs show agreement with **number** (singular or plural):

| | | |
|---|---|---|
| 22a. | *Aida <u>drives</u> to work every day.* | singular |
| 22b. | *Aida and Rahman <u>drive</u> nice cars.* | plural |

Finally, finite verbs show agreement with **person** (first, second or third person pronoun):

| | | |
|---|---|---|
| 23a. | *I <u>am</u> eager to start writing.* | first person |
| 23b. | *You <u>are</u> very busy, aren't you?* | second person |
| 23c. | *Michelle <u>is</u> a good friend of mine.* | third person |

**Non-finite Verbs**

The **non-finite imperative** verb is used to make requests and commands. They take the base form and generally appear at the start of sentences with the doer/agent of the action not mentioned (but it is always the understood second person pronoun *you*):

| | |
|---|---|
| 24. | *<u>Give</u> me your money!* |
| 25. | *<u>Brush</u> your teeth!* |

A verb that is formed with an infinitive "to" is known as a **to-infinitive**. These infinitives are also non-finite, i.e. they do not show tense and agreement:

26. *Yesterday, Jimmy said he decided <u>to buy</u> tickets to the concert.*
27. *Mary wants <u>to go</u> home.*

In sentence 26, the verb *buy* does not contain tense (it happened *yesterday*), and in sentence 27, the non-finite verb *go* does not show agreement with number (*Mary* is singular, i.e. one person).

The **bare infinitives** are sometimes described as the infinitives without *to*. They generally appear after **causative verbs** (verbs that cause something else to happen) like *help, make, let*, and **verbs of perception** like *hear, see* and *watch*.

28. *Please help me <u>download</u> the lectures.*
29. *I saw him <u>climb</u> over the wall.*

Some grammarians also refer to the verbs that appear after modal verbs like *can, would,* and *must* as the bare infinitive:

30. *Susan must <u>eat</u> chicken rice every week or she'll get very upset.*

Consider the following pair of sentences and decide if the verb form is similar or different – perform or performed:

*I had the chance to see a famous singer _____ on stage yesterday.*
*I had the chance to see how a famous singer _____ on stage yesterday.*

We need the bare infinitive *perform* in the first sentence, and the past tense *performed* in the second. But why is this so? Try substituting the noun phrase *the famous singer* with a pronoun, and you'll immediately notice the difference between the two sentences:

*I had the chance to see her (perform) on stage yesterday.*
*I had the chance to see how she (performed) on stage yesterday.*

### Grammar Detective

State if the underlined verbs are finite or non-finite, and identify the verb form.

i.    Diane <u>plays</u> the piano.
ii.   The children <u>broke</u> the window.
iii.  <u>Run</u> to work every day!
iv.   It took courage to <u>continue</u> after the accident.
v.    <u>Leaving</u> home can be very exciting.
vi.   Here are answers to questions <u>asked</u> by my grammar teacher.
vii.  You can help me <u>cook</u> dinner.

## VERB PHRASES

We will now look at how verbs can form verb phrases and how to label them.

**Verb phrases**, also known as **verb groups**, are groups of verbs that go together and function as one unit. In this book, we do not make a distinction between verb phrases and verb groups. The main/lexical verb gives the verb phrase its meaning and the auxiliary verbs give grammatical information such as tense, agreement and aspect.

The table below illustrates the structure of a verb phrase.

| | Auxiliary Verb(s) | | | Main/ Lexical Verb |
|---|---|---|---|---|
| Modal | Primary | | | |
| | Perfective HAVE | Progressive/ Continuous BE | Passive BE | |
| e.g. *can, could, will, would, shall, should, may, might, must, have to* | e.g. *have, had, has* **+ -ed/en** | e.g. *be, been, is, was, were* **+ -ing** | e.g. *be, been, being* **+ -ed/en** | e.g. *try, tries, tried, trying* |
| *should* | *have* | *been* | | *driving* |

There are two kinds of auxiliary verbs: **modal auxiliary verbs** and **primary auxiliary verbs**. In the table, *HAVE, BE* and *BE* are set in capitals to indicate "any appropriate form of this verb". Let's now see how we can use the table to analyse a verb phrase like *should have been driving*.

- The main verb that carries the meaning of the verb phrase is *driving*. Note that only the main verb is obligatory while all auxiliary verbs, modal or primary, are optional.
- *Should* is a modal verb. In most varieties of English, a verb phrase can take only one modal auxiliary verb.
- There are two primary auxiliary verbs, *have* and *been*, and they go

into the respective columns, perfective and progressive. How do we tell if the auxiliary verb is progressive or passive? We look at the next verb – we find *driving* with the *-ing* participle; hence, we place *been* in the progressive *BE* column. Again, only one primary auxiliary verb can go into each column.

It is quite rare for all five slots to be filled. In *The car will have been being driven for eight hours now*, every single slot is filled. The verb contains the following parts:

- *will*     modal auxiliary
- *have*     perfective *HAVE* (+ *-ed/en* on the following verb)
- *been*     progressive *BE* (+ *-ing* on the following verb)
- *being*     passive *BE* (+ *-ed/en* on the following verb)
- *driven*     main verb

However, many speakers of English may find this sentence somewhat strange and non-standard (preferring the more natural-sounding *will have been driven*).

In a verb phrase, the first verb is typically finite and the rest are non-finite. After the modal *will*, the appropriate (non-finite) form of the perfective *HAVE* is *have*. It adds *-ed/en* to the following progressive *BE* verb, giving us *been*. Since this is the progressive auxiliary verb, it then adds *-ing* to the next verb. The passive *BE* therefore takes the form *being*, and to signal passive voice, it adds *-ed/en* to the last verb in the verb phrase, which is the main verb *driven*.

## Tense and Aspect

Auxiliary verbs and suffixes on verbs like *-ed* and *-s* convey information about tense and aspect. As mentioned above, there are only two **tenses** in English – present and past.

**Aspect** refers to the way we should view an action or a process. The **perfective (or perfect) aspect**, which uses the perfective *HAVE* auxiliary, is used to relate to an action or fact that began at some time in the past and is still true or relevant at the time of speaking, or was recently completed:

31.  *Tim <u>has seen</u> a ghost.* (a true statement i.e. a fact, whether it happened last week or a year ago)
32.  *The children <u>have</u> just <u>left</u> for school.* (recently completed event)

The **progressive or continuous aspect**, which uses the progressive *BE* auxiliary, refers to ongoing events. Compare *Jane is singing* with *Jane was singing*. Both sentences tell us that *singing* was ongoing; it went on for some time, i.e. an event with duration. *Is* tells us it is happening at the present and *was*, that it was ongoing at a past time.

When a verb phrase has no perfective or progressive aspect, then it is considered **simple**, as seen in the examples below:

33.  *The girls <u>sent</u> a card to Santa.*
34.  *A card <u>was sent</u> to Santa.*

## Voice: Active and Passive

Another important distinction to make between verbs is whether they are active or passive. In the **active voice**, the subject of the sentence is the doer or agent of the action:

35a. *The angry penguins <u>attacked</u> my best friend.*

When the verb is in the **passive voice**, the subject of the sentence is the patient or undergoer of the action, and the *BE* auxiliary is used. The doer or agent of the action can optionally be added to the end of the sentence in the *by*-phrase, as seen in:

35b. *My best friend <u>was attacked</u> (by the angry penguins).*

**Active voice**

The angry penguins attacked my best friend.

**Passive voice**

My best friend <u>was attacked</u> (by the penguins).

When we use the active voice, the subject of the sentence is seen as *actively* carrying out the action described, and in the passive voice, the subject is passively *undergoing* the action. Passive sentences allow us to avoid referring to the agent – the *by*-phrase containing the doer of the action is optional.

Bear in mind that active and passive are types of *voice*, not aspect. We will take a more detailed look at active and passive verb forms/sentences in Chapter 6.

## Modal Auxiliary Verbs

Modals help us indicate **modality**, which is the speaker's indication of certainty, possibility, permission, obligation, necessity, volition (intention to act), etc. While modals are always finite, they do not have *-s* or *-ed* forms. When we consider this pair of modals – *can* vs *could* – we are likely to think that the difference between the two lies in the tense. However, consider these pairs of sentences:

36a. *I can take that grammar class now.*

36b. *I could take that grammar class now.*

37a. *I can take that grammar class next year.*

37b. *I could take that grammar class next year.*

Clearly, the difference is not one of tense. These days, pairs of modals like *can/could* are rarely used to show tense distinctions. As seen in examples above, the difference between the (a) and (b) sentences has nothing to do with tense. Historically, *can/could, will/would, shall/should* and *may/might* were present and past tense pairs. This distinction is still useful when we are talking about what someone can do (now in the present time) or could (in the past):

38. *She could run 10 kilometres without breaking a sweat when she was a teenager, but now, in her 40s, she can barely run a kilometre without stopping multiple times to catch her breath.*

Modals are also useful when we transform direct speech to indirect/reported speech as seen in this pair of examples:

39a. *Jimmy told Mary, "I can help you with your project."*
(direct speech)

39b. *Jimmy told Mary that he could help her with her project.*
(indirect/reported speech)

We will discuss direct and indirect/reported speech in greater detail in Chapter 6.

So if a modal is not used to show tense, then what do modals do? Modal verbs indicate modality and they are linked to different meanings. Some of these are illustrated below:

- Possibility: *They <u>may</u> take the train to Jurong; It <u>could</u> be cold in winter.*
- Ability: *Jimmy <u>can</u> drive really well.*
- Permission: *You <u>may</u> sit next to me if you wish to; <u>Could</u> I ask a question please?*
- Obligation: *I <u>should</u>/<u>must</u> take care of my parents when they grow old.*
- Probability: *The students <u>will</u>/<u>might</u> submit their homework by this afternoon.*

Let's consider the difference in meaning between these pairs of modals:

## May vs Might

We use *may/might* to refer to something that is possible, but uncertain. *Might* suggests a weaker possibility compared to *may*:

40a.  *She <u>may</u> be at home.* (maybe a 50% chance)
40b.  *Amy <u>might</u> be there too.* (a smaller chance)

## Can vs Could

The pair of modals *can/could* are used to refer to the possibility of something taking place, and to refer to someone's ability. *Could* suggests a weaker possibility compared to *can*. When it is used to refer to ability, *could* is used to refer to someone's past ability, while *can* refers to a present ability. When referred to possibility:

41a.  *Swimming immediately after eating <u>can</u> be dangerous.* (certain)
41b.  *There's a bad traffic jam on the expressway. That <u>could</u> explain why he's late.* (less certain)

When *can/could* are used to refer to ability:

42a.  *She <u>can</u> drive any car.* (present)
42b.  *When he was younger, he <u>could</u> run faster than any of us.* (past)

## Will vs Would

The modal *will* refers to something that is more definite, while *would* is more tentative:

43a.   *We <u>will</u> go fishing.*
43b.   *We <u>would</u> go fishing if the weather was good.* (it is conditional)

When making a request or an offer, *would* is considered more polite than *will*:

44a.   *<u>Would</u> you please help me carry these heavy boxes?* (request)
44b.   *<u>Would</u> you like to join us for dinner?* (offer)

## Shall vs Should

The modal *shall* is used to make an offer and to express certain laws and rules:

45a.   *<u>Shall</u> I get you a cup of coffee?* (offer)
45b.   *Students <u>shall</u> remain in their seats until all the papers have been collected.* (rule)

*Should*, on the other hand, is used to give a suggestion or to talk about the right thing to do in a situation:

46.   *You <u>should</u> exercise every day.*

Here are more examples for you to consider. Notice the differences in meaning between *shall* and *should*, all of which are not connected to tense:

*I shall go home now.*
- I have made a decision. I am going to go home now. I am just letting you know.
- The modal *will* is also possible here.

*I should go home now.*
- It is a good idea, but maybe I will stay longer. A suggestion to myself.

*You shall do what I tell you.*
- I am commanding/ordering you to do what I tell you to do. *Will* is also possible here.

*You should do what I tell you.*
- I am giving you strong advice.

Now consider the difference in meaning when you use these following pairs of modals:

## Should vs Must

*Should* is used to make a suggestion, and to offer advice or an opinion. *Must*, on the other hand, is used to convey a stronger suggestion, or an order:

47a.  *You <u>should</u> stop smoking because it's bad for you.*
47b.  *You <u>must</u> stop smoking or you'll die.*

Sometimes *must* refers to a strong belief: *She <u>must</u> be over 90 years old.*

## Shall vs Will

For some of us, when we were in primary school, our teachers may have shared this rule in class: Use *shall* with first person pronouns like *I* or *we* to express future events, and for all other pronouns like *they* or *he*, use *will*:

48a.  *I <u>shall</u> bake tomorrow.*
48b.  *She <u>will</u> bake tomorrow.*

This is considered an outdated rule. In modern English, there is no difference in meaning between *shall* and *will* when referring to the simple future. There is also no restriction on using the first person pronoun *I* with *will*.

In English, there are combinations of words that are modal-like because they also indicate modality and convey meanings similar to "true modals". These are called **semi-modals** or **marginal modals**. Some examples include *have to, be able to, be about to, be going to, be supposed to, dare, need, ought to,* and *used to.* Consider the semi-modal *have to.* It is synonymous with *must,* and it is the alternative that we need to use if we would like to convey the past tense since *must* does not have a past tense form: *We must/had to study.*

## Primary Auxiliary Verbs

There are three primary auxiliary verbs in English — "have", "be" and "do". While modal verbs only function as auxiliary verbs, "have", "be" and "do" can be auxiliary or main verbs. They are main verbs when they are at the end of the verb phrase (*will <u>have</u>, is <u>doing</u>*), and they are auxiliary verbs when they precede main verbs (<u>*have*</u> *slept, <u>is</u> eating*). We have already looked at the perfective *HAVE* auxiliary and the progressive and passive *BE* auxiliaries. Missing from the table on page 90 was "do", which is used for emphasis, and to form negatives and questions:

49. *I do mean what I said to you earlier.* (emphatic "do")
50. *My sister does not want the same tuition teacher next year.* (dummy "do" to form a negative)
51. *Does he know why you made him sit in the corner?* (dummy "do" to form a question)

The "do" auxiliary is used to form negatives and questions. This is referred to as the *do*-support. The auxiliary is needed because English has changed and lost the option of phrasing both respectively as *My sister wants the same tuition teacher next year not* and *Know he why you made him sit in the corner?* – which may have been possible in old/Elizabethan English.

## Naming a Verb Phrase

It is useful to be able to label or name verb phrases according to tense, modality, aspect and voice in order to discuss the various uses of each combination, or explaining why a certain combination is not appropriate in a particular context (which will be covered in the next section, **Using the Different Verb Types**).

To label a verb phrase, we use the following table:

| Verb Phrase | Finiteness | Modality, Tense, Aspect | Voice |
|---|---|---|---|
|  |  |  |  |

Firstly, we label the auxiliaries, and we do so from left to right, according to the information they convey. Consider the example below:

52. *Jennifer has been going to Iceland for years.*

In this sentence, *has* is perfective; *been* is progressive; and *going* is the main verb. The perfective *HAVE* takes the finite form *has* here to show agreement with time (present) and number (singular *Jennifer*). It then transfers the *-en* suffix onto the following verb, making it *been*. The perfective aspect tells us that the act of going started in the past and continues to the present. Next, the progressive *been* transfers the *-ing* suffix to the main verb *going* to show that this is an ongoing event with duration. Since the subject of the sentence *Jennifer* is the doer/agent of the action, the verb is active. Hence a complete description for the verb phrase is:

| Verb Phrase | Finiteness | Modality, Tense, Aspect | Voice |
|---|---|---|---|
| *has been going* | finite | present perfect(ive) progressive | active |

Let's consider another example:

53.  *Sally <u>must</u> <u>have</u> <u>been</u> <u>scolded</u> by her mother.*

In this sentence, *must* is the modal; *have* is perfective; *been* is passive; and *scolded* is the main verb. The modal *must* shows that the speaker is very certain that Sally was scolded by her mother. After *must*, the perfective *HAVE* takes the non-finite form *have*, and it transfers the *-en* suffix onto the following verb, making it *been*. The perfective tells us that the act of scolding is completed at the time of speaking. Then, the passive *been* transfers the *-ed* suffix to the main verb *scolded*.

Since the verb phrase begins with a modal, it is finite. Note that while all modals are finite, we do not indicate its tense. It is sufficient to indicate "modal" in the "Modality, Tense, Aspect" column.  A complete description for the verb phrase is as follows:

| Verb Phrase | Finiteness | Modality, Tense, Aspect | Voice |
|---|---|---|---|
| *must have been scolded* | finite | modal perfective | passive |

Now consider the following pair of sentences:

54a.  *Peter <u>drew</u> a picture of the Eiffel Tower last week.*
54b.  *A picture of the Eiffel Tower <u>was drawn</u> by Peter last week.*

| Verb Phrase | Finiteness | Modality, Tense, Aspect | Voice |
|---|---|---|---|
| 54a *drew* | finite | simple past | active |
| 54b *was drawn* | finite | simple past | passive |

The difference between 54a and 54b is only in terms of voice. In 54a, the subject *Peter* is also the doer/agent of the action *drew,* while in 54b, the subject *A picture of the Eiffel Tower* is the patient or undergoer of the action. Both verb groups do not show modality or aspect (i.e. no modal auxiliaries, and no perfective *HAVE* or progressive *BE*). But there is tense – both verbs refer to past events. Hence the "Modality, Tense, Aspect" column is simply marked "simple past".

Let us now consider the sentences below:

55a.  *Mike <u>played</u> computer games for four hours.*
55b.  *Mike <u>will</u> <u>have</u> <u>been</u> <u>playing</u> computer games for four hours now.*
55c.  *<u>Playing</u> computer games for four hours made Mike too exhausted to complete his homework.*

| Verb Phrase | Finiteness | Modality, Tense, Aspect | Voice |
|---|---|---|---|
| 55a *played* | finite | simple past | active |
| 55b *will have been playing* | finite | modal perfect(ive) progressive | active |
| 55c *Playing* | non-finite | progressive | active |

55c contains a non-finite verb phrase *playing* which contains the *-ing* progressive aspect, but does not have tense or agreement.

Take a look at the following sentences:

56. *Tom has never been thanked for his help.*
57. *Marianne is not attending the cooking class tonight.*
58. *Did you see the new airplane at the airport?*
59. *We can choose to discuss this matter calmly instead of arguing about it.*

| Verb phrase | | Finiteness | Modality, Tense, Aspect | Voice |
|---|---|---|---|---|
| 56 | *has ... been thanked* | finite | present perfect(ive) | passive |
| 57 | *is ... attending* | finite | present progressive | active |
| 58 | *Did ... see* | finite | simple past | active |
| 59 | *can choose* | finite | simple modal | active |
| | *to discuss* | non-finite | — | active |
| | *arguing* | non-finite | progressive | active |

Examples 56 and 57 show that verb phrases may be split by an intervening adverb like *never, not* and *already.* So what we need to do is to identify only the verbs (by doing a word-class analysis of all the words in the sentence). When we form yes-no questions in English, as seen in 58, the verb phrase is split into two parts because of the subject-auxiliary inversion (i.e. the auxiliary *did* and the subject *you* swap places). Sentence 59 contains three verb phrases. The verb phrase *can choose* is labelled as "simple modal" because there is no aspect (no perfective and no progressive). The *to*-infinitive, *to go,* contains no modal, tense or aspect, and so we put a dash or line through this column to show that we know that none of these applies. Finally, the verb phrase *arguing* is a non-finite verb that contains no tense, but it has the progressive aspect. For all the three verbs in 59, the doer or agent of the actions is the subject *We,* making the voice active.

## Grammar Detective

Each sentence below contains at least one verb phrase. Identify *ALL the verb phrases* in all five sentences and complete the table to show the finiteness, tense, aspect, modality and voice.

*(i) I visited Iceland in winter several years ago as I was then researching a book on global happiness. (ii) What was this country, adrift in the freezing North Atlantic, doing at the top the world's happiness rankings? (iii) According to a recent United Nations report on world happiness, happiness is evenly distributed in Iceland, which has to mean that most Icelanders are more or less equally happy. (iv) Icelanders have developed a fierce resilience honed over centuries of deprivation and isolation. (v) Just think of winter darkness, volcanic eruptions and unforgiving terrain so otherworldly that NASA were prepared to dispatch the Apollo astronauts here in 1965 to train for their upcoming moon walks.*

Adapted from http://www.bbc.com/travel/story/20160509-the-truth-about-icelandic-happiness

|  | Verb Phrase | Finiteness | Modality, Tense, Aspect | Voice |
|---|---|---|---|---|
| i |  |  |  |  |
| ii |  |  |  |  |
| iii |  |  |  |  |
| iv |  |  |  |  |
| v |  |  |  |  |

## Using the Different Verb Types

In this section, we consider the context of use for all the verb phrases.

The **simple present** is used to convey the following information:

| Factual Present | Habitual Present | Instantaneous Present | Historic Present | Planned Future Events |
|---|---|---|---|---|
| Used to state facts about the world. This is often called the "timeless present". | Used to state actions that are repeated habitually. | Used to provide an instantaneous sense of the present, especially in reporting live events like sports commentaries, or in story-telling. | Used to state past events as if they were the present, e.g. in the telling of stories and jokes. The present tense for past is also common in headlines. | Used to refer to the future time, normally to a pre-determined or planned course of action. |
| *The earth is round.* | *I visit the library every Friday.* | *Jimmy throws the ball to Ronald, who then passes it to Beckham.*<br><br>*The feeble old man staggers to his feet and grabs hold of his son's hand.* | *Japanese Prime Minister resigns.*<br><br>*A large bear attacks the camper.* | *My flight arrives tomorrow at 12 noon.* |

The **simple past** is used in the following contexts:

| Past Event | Hypothetical Future | Indirect / Reported Speech |
|---|---|---|
| Used to refer to events that took place at a specific point in the past, especially with specific time expressions. | Used to refer to both the present time as well as the hypothetical future. | Used in indirect or reported speech even though the event referred to might be in the present time in direct speech. |
| *Jenny <u>visited</u> us last month.* | *I wish I <u>had</u> more time.*<br><br>*If I <u>had</u> a million dollars, I <u>would</u> help you pay off your loan.* | *She said, "It is cold."*<br>*She said that it <u>was</u> cold.* |

The simple past is used to refer to many types of past events: short, quickly finished actions/happenings; longer situations; and repeated actions:

60. *Mom <u>cut</u> her finger yesterday.*  (quickly finished action)
61. *I <u>spent</u> my entire youth doing nothing.*  (longer past event)
62. *Regularly every school break, Jane <u>worked</u> at McDonald's.*
    (repeated past action)

   This verb form is common in narratives and descriptions of past events. To talk about past events, the simple past is generally used, unless there is a special reason for using one of the other tenses/aspects.

The **present progressive/continuous** is used in the following scenarios:

| "Around now" | Repeated Actions | The Future |
|---|---|---|
| Used to refer to temporary events that are going on now or "around now". | Used to refer to repeated events, if these are happening around the moment of speaking. | Used to refer to future events that have some present reality. Common in discussions of personal arrangements and fixed plans. |
| *Hurry up! We are waiting for you!*<br><br>*He is working in London at the moment.* | *I am travelling a lot these days.*<br>(compare with the simple present: *I go to the mountains twice a year,* which is used to refer to a habitual action.) | *What are you doing this evening?*<br>*I am watching a movie.*<br><br>*My car is going in for a service next week.* |

The **present progressive** is not used to talk about permanent situations, or about things that happen regularly, or all the time:

63.   *That bear is eating your breakfast.*
64.   *What do bears eat?*

    **What are bears eating?* cannot be used to ask about the (habitual) diet of bears as the present progressive is more appropriate for asking about an action going on at the moment of speaking.

Think about the difference in meaning when we use the present continuous vs the simple present:

Event:
- *He blows his whistle.* (a brief blast)
- *He is blowing his whistle.* (continuous or repeated)

State:
- *We <u>live</u> in Italy.* (permanently)
- *We <u>are living</u> in Italy.* (at present)

Habitual:
- *He <u>writes</u> his own programs.* (regularly)
- *He <u>is writing</u> his own programs.* (as a temporary measure)

The **past progressive/continuous** verb form is used in the following contexts:

| Ongoing Past | "Backgrounding" Past Events |
| --- | --- |
| Used to say that something was in progress around a particular past time. | Used together with simple past, the past continuous refers to the longer "background" event or the action that was interrupted by another past action. |
| *When the student left school yesterday, the sun <u>was setting</u> and the sky <u>was getting</u> dark.* | *The phone rang while he <u>was eating</u> dinner.* |

subject + was / were + verb + ing

He <u>was eating</u> dinner when the phone rang.

7pm - 7:20pm                    7:15pm

The **present perfect** is used in the following contexts:

| Relevance to Present | Recently Completed | Unknown Time |
|---|---|---|
| Used to refer to an action which began in the past and has continued to the present. | Used to refer to an action that has just been completed. | Used to refer to an action which took place in the past but when exactly in the past is not significant or not mentioned. |
| We _have lived_ in Bedok for 10 years. | The children _have_ just _finished_ their meal. | I _have misplaced_ my wallet. |

The **past perfect**, on the other hand, is used in these contexts:

| Past of the Past | Reported Speech | Unreal Situations |
|---|---|---|
| Used when stating an event that took place prior to another event in the past. The past perfect is used to refer to the first of two past actions. | Used in reported speech as the past equivalent of the present perfect verb used in direct speech. | Used in unreal situations to talk about past events that did not happen. |
| The bank _had been robbed_ by the time the police arrived. | John said, "I have sent the books to Mary". (direct speech) John said that he _had sent_ the books to Mary. (indirect speech) | If I _had been_ able to decide for myself, I would have studied medicine instead of linguistics. |

According to some grammarians, when we include time conjunctions like _after_ and _as soon as_, the past perfect is not necessary:

65.  After it _got_ dark, we went home.
66.  As soon as Jane _arrived_, we had our meal.

Consider this pair of sentences with the **simple past** and **present perfect** verbs. Note the difference in meaning:

*We <u>studied</u> enough to pass the exam.*  → The exam is over.
*We <u>have studied</u> enough to pass the exam.*  → The exam is still to come.

Similarly, when we use the present perfect verb *have arrived* in this sentence, *You <u>have arrived</u> late to work three times this month,* it must mean that this month is not over yet. Thus, this event is relevant to the present time. However, if we refer to how many times you showed up late last month, we use the simple past, as seen in *You <u>arrived</u> late to work three times last month.*

The **present perfect progressive/continuous** verb is used in the following situations:

| Events with Present Results | Repeated Event with Duration | How Long? |
|---|---|---|
| Used to refer to events which have just stopped but have present results. | Used to refer to repeated, continuous activities. | Used to refer to an event that had been going on for some time. |
| *I am so sorry that I'm late. <u>Have</u> you <u>been waiting</u> long?* | *My students' parents <u>have been calling</u> me all day.* | *How long <u>have</u> you <u>been teaching</u>?* |

The **past perfect progressive/continuous** has these two contexts of use:

| Past of the Past | How Long? |
| --- | --- |
| Used to refer to events that had continued up to the past moment that we are thinking about or shortly before it. | Used to refer to an event that went on for some time in the past before another past event took place. |
| *When I found Mary, I could see that she <u>had been crying</u>.* | *When she arrived, she <u>had been travelling</u> for over twenty hours.* |

### Grammar Detective

In this chapter, we have discussed the different classification of verbs including the verb forms, the naming/labelling of verbs, and the contexts of use. Drawing on what we have discussed, choose the most appropriate answer:

i.  Jason wanted to help Mindy with her homework but Gavin _____ already _____ it.
    (a)  had...did          (c)  have...done
    (b)  has...did          (d)  had...done

ii. Jimmy _____ in a university in Boston since last year and will only move back to Singapore in two years' time.
    (a)  studied            (c)  has been studying
    (b)  has studied        (d)  had been studying

iii. My best friend made me _____ across the drain
to get to the playground.
(a)  jump                 (c)  jumped
(b)  jumps                (d)  jumping


iv. "Has anyone ever _____ on live television before?"
J-Lo asked the American Idol participants.
(a)  sing                 (c)  sung
(b)  sang                 (d)  sings


v. Mr Lim, together with his students, _____ in the
school hall before their performance yesterday.
(a)  rehearse             (c)  rehearsed
(b)  have rehearsed       (d)  had rehearsed

**Clause structure**

# CHAPTER FIVE

# CLAUSES, SVOCA ANALYSIS, CLAUSE AND SENTENCE TYPES

We began by looking at words in Chapter 2, and then moved on to combining them to form phrases in Chapters 3 and 4. In this chapter, we will expand these further into clauses and sentences.

**CLAUSES**

Clauses are built around verb phrases, and each clause must minimally contain the participants that the verb requires for the clause to be grammatical, and the meaning of the verb complete. If we choose to, we could add additional details, but these are optional and referred to as circumstances.

Let us consider the different ways we can look at clauses.

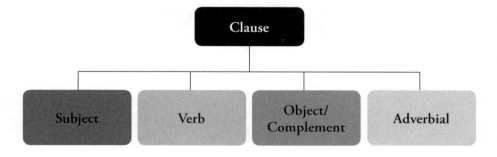

## Meaning, Form and Function

Consider this sentence: *Iman enjoys his grammar classes now*. If we consider the parts that make up the sentence, we can separate it into four — each part is a constituent or a standalone, meaningful unit that takes the form of a word or a phrase, and each constituent can be substituted with a question word:

1.   | *Iman* | *enjoys* | *his grammar classes* | *now*. |
     who   enjoys          what          when

We can unpack this sentence in three different ways:

   I. In terms of the **meaning** of each constituent, we have:
- **processes**, which tell us what is happening: *enjoys*
- **participants**, which tell us who/what is/are involved: *Iman, his grammar classes*
- **circumstances**, which tell us the why/where/how/when/etc. of the process: *now*

   II. In terms of the **form** of each meaningful constituent:
- **noun, noun phrase**: *Iman, his grammar classes*
- **verb**: *enjoys*
- **adverb**: *now*

   III. Each constituent in the clause can also be analysed in terms of its **function**:
- **S**ubject: *Iman*
- **V**erb: *enjoys*
- **O**bject: *his grammar classes*
- **A**dverbial: *now*

## Verbs and Clause Patterns

Since clauses are built around verbs and verb phrases, if there is only one verb (phrase) in a sentence, then there is only one clause. In the sentence, *Belinda wants to go to Italy,* there are two clauses since there are two verbs/verb phrases: *wants* and *to go.* Each verb (phrase) produces a different type of clause depending on the participants that it requires for the meaning of the clause to be complete. The number of participants in a clause depends on the main verb of each verb phrase, and not the auxiliary verb. Participants are obligatory elements in a clause. Adverbials are not participants, because unlike participants, adverbials are usually optional.

There are five classes of verbs, and each one takes a different type and number of participants. Consider the examples below. The main verbs are in bold, while the compulsory participants or constituents are underlined.

## Verbs that Require Only One Participant

**Intransitive verbs** take only one participant, i.e. a Subject, with a clause structure of S + V (Subject + Verb):

2.   *Homer* is **drooling**.
       S          V

3.   *Aida* **speaks** *confidently.*
       S      V        A

The adverbial *confidently* which tells us how Aida speaks is not a constituent; it is optional. The Subject, *Aida,* however, is not optional and without it, the clause is ungrammatical (*\*Speaks confidently*).

## Verbs that Require Two Participants

**Transitive verbs** take two participants, i.e. a Subject and an Object, with the clause structure S + V + O (Subject + Verb + Object):

4.  *The children* **built** *sandcastles*.
        S          V        O

5.  *Matthew's mother* **baked** *some cookies*.
        S              V        O

**Copular** or **linking verbs** also require two participants, i.e. a Subject and a Subject Complement, with a clause structure of S + V + Cs (Subject + Verb + Subject Complement). There are some copular or linking verbs that take a compulsory Adverbial, with the structure S + V + A (Subject + Verb + Adverbial):

6.  *Rahman* **was** *a banker*.
        S      V      Cs

7.  *Rahman* **appears** *extremely tired*.
        S        V            Cs

8.  *Rahman* **is** *at work*.
        S      V      A

Although adverbials are usually optional, note that if the adverbial *at work* is left out of the sentence, the resulting sentence *\*Rahman is* ends up being ungrammatical. Even though it is obligatory, it is still not a participant.

## Verbs that Require Three Participants

**Ditransitive verbs** are verbs that take three participants: a Subject, Indirect Object (Oi) and Direct Object (Od), with the clause structure S + V+ Oi + Od (Subject + Verb + Indirect Object + Direct Object):

9.  *Margaret* **sent** *Jenny* *a belated birthday gift*.
        S        V      Oi          Od

10. _His father_ **bought** _him_ _a new laptop_.
      S       V     Oi     Od

If the Direct Object comes first, we use a preposition together with the Indirect Object, and the prepositional phrase _for him_ in the sentence below is called a "prepositional object":

11. _His father_ **bought** _a new laptop_ _for him_.
      S      V     Od       Oi

**Complex-transitive verbs** also require three participants: a Subject, Object, and an Object Complement, giving us the clause structure S + V + O + Co (Subject + Verb + Object + Object Complement):

12. _Mariam_ **made** _Peter_ _the school's English language ambassador_.
      S     V    O            Co

13. _We_ **told** _the taxi driver_ _to drive faster_.
      S  V     O        Co

Consider this sentence:

_I will appreciate if you would reply by tonight._

Do you think there is anything wrong with it?

The verb _appreciate_ is a transitive verb which takes two compulsory participants: a Subject and an Object. The sentence _I will appreciate if you would reply by tonight_ is clearly missing the Object (what will I appreciate?). The _if_-clause (_if you would reply by_ tonight) is not the object; it is called the conditional clause, which functions as an adverbial. Thus, a

> better way to phrase the sentence is by including an object which can take the form of a pronoun or a noun phrase:
>
> *I would* **appreciate** *it if you would reply by tonight.* (pronoun)
> *I would* **appreciate** *your reply by tonight.* (noun phrase)

## Different Uses of Verbs

Some verbs have different uses. In 1a and 1b, the verb *eat*, for example, can be used as an intransitive or a transitive verb; and in 2a, 2b and 2c, the verb *made* can be transitive, ditransitive or complex-transitive:

14a. *Have … you … eaten?* (intransitive)
     V    S    V

14b. *You ate the entire pie!* (transitive)
     S    V    O

15a. *Fazilah made the gorgeous cake.* (transitive)
     S      V       O

15b. *Fazilah made us the gorgeous cake.* (ditransitive)
     S      V    Oi      Od

15c. *Fazilah made us look like amateurs.* (complex-transitive)
     S      V    O    Co

# SVOCA (SUBJECT, VERB, OBJECT, COMPLEMENT, ADVERBIAL) ANALYSIS

We will now take a closer look at each type of constituent according to its form and function in the clause. Form refers to what a word or constituent is: for example, the word class (noun, adjective), the type of phrase (noun phrase, prepositional phrase), and the type of clause (finite/non-finite subordinate clause). The labels – S, V, O, C, A – are function labels because they tell us what each constituent is doing in the clause. Other labels for function include premodifer/postmodifier of head noun, and head of noun phrase.

To illustrate, consider the clause structure of the sentence *The boy with the silly name hates being made fun of:*

|  | *The boy with the silly name* | *hates* | *being made fun of.* |
|---|---|---|---|
| **Form** | noun phrase | verb | non-finite subordinate clause |
| **Function** | S | V | O |

Now, let's look closely at each function label, and identify the different forms those functions labels can take.

## Subject

English is a language with the word order Subject-Verb-Object (SVO). The Subject is typically the first constituent in a sentence, and precedes the Verb. In active sentences, the Subject is the agent or doer of the verb/action, whereas in passive sentences, the Subject is the patient or undergoer of the action described by the verb:

16a. *The girl* ***chased*** *some butterflies.* (active: the girl is the agent/doer)
     S    V       O

16b. *The butterflies* ***were chased*** *by the girl.* (passive: the butterflies is
       S       V         A    the patient/undergoer)

In main clauses, the verb agrees with the Subject, and not with the Object, hence *The boy likes the apples* (singular verb to agree with singular S) is grammatical but not \**The boy like the apples*. The Subject can take the following forms:

| Noun Phrase/ Pronoun | [**Your former employer/She**] smiled at me. |
|---|---|
| Finite Subordinate Clause | [**That he will be late again**] should be obvious to everyone. |
| Non-finite Subordinate Clause | [**To become a great cook**] takes lots of practice. |

Subordinate clauses may function as the Subject, a role usually played by nouns, pronouns and noun phrases. When we have a subordinate clause as Subject, it is considered to be grammatically singular. Such subordinate clauses, like the one underlined in the example below, are sometimes called **noun clauses** as they usually answer *who/what* questions:

17. *Being caught in a massive traffic jam* ***is*** *a real pain*.
                S                     V   Cs

Sometimes, Adverbials of location are inverted with the Subject. This is termed as "locative inversion". Consider the following examples:

18a. *Inside the house* ***are*** *two angry birds*.
       A        V       S

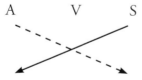

18b. *Two angry birds* ***are*** *inside the house.*
       S       V       A

The Adverbial may be found at the beginning of the sentence, in the Subject position, like in the first sentence, but that does not make it the Subject. This is because the verb does not agree with the phrase *inside the house*. The verb agrees with the "real" Subject *two angry birds*. Did you know that locative inversion is very common in children's stories?

## Verb

If you still remember, we count clauses by counting verbs. In a sentence with one or many clauses, there is at least one main clause. In a main clause, there is a main verb that tells us what the clause or sentence is about. This is the Verb. Although we refer to it as the Verb (V), it may be a verb phrase which contains just the main verb or a main verb preceded by one or several auxiliary verbs. The term "verb phrase" refers to the form, whereas V is a function label. Hence, we can talk about a verb phrase functioning as, or doing the job of, the V in a clause.

## Object

Because English is an SVO language, the Object typically follows the Verb:

19. <u>You</u>  **can trust**  <u>some people</u>.
    S        V          O

In some contexts, the object is fronted — it appears at the beginning of the sentence and receives emphasis or prominence: for example, <u>Some people</u> you can trust.

### Direct Object (Od) and Indirect Object (Oi)

If a clause has only one Object, it is, by default, the **Direct Object** (Od). Ditransitive verbs take an **Indirect Object** and a Direct Object. The Direct Object is the one that is directly affected by the action — for instance, it gets passed around. The Indirect Object generally refers to the recipient of the Direct Object. In the section on **Verbs that Require Three Participants**, we saw that in most ditransitive verbs, the Indirect Object comes before the Direct Object, as seen in 20a. However, it is possible for the Direct Object to precede the Indirect Object with the latter taking the form of a prepositional phrase like the example in 20b:

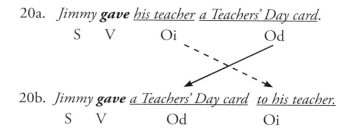

20a. *Jimmy **gave** <u>his teacher</u> <u>a Teachers' Day card</u>*.
      S    V     Oi         Od

20b. *Jimmy **gave** <u>a Teachers' Day card</u> <u>to his teacher.</u>*
      S    V      Od       Oi

The Object can take the following forms:

| | |
|---|---|
| Noun Phrase/ Pronoun | *We bought [a new computer/it].* |
| Finite Subordinate Clause | *I know [that he is guilty of murder].* |
| Non-finite Subordinate Clause | *She hopes [to bake cookies this weekend].* |

# Complement

Complements are constituents needed to complete the clause. There are two types of complements: the subject complement and the object complement.

## Subject Complement (Cs)

**Subject Complements** (Cs) complete the clause by giving information about the Subject, and hence, they are distinct from Objects. Subject Complements also tend to pair with copular or linking verbs, while Objects come after transitive verbs:

21a. *Jimmy **is** an English teacher.*
     S    V       Cs

21b. *Jimmy **became** very famous.*
      S     V       Cs

As we have already discussed in the section on **Verbs that Require Two Participants**, linking or copular verbs may also be followed by compulsory adverbials. In the sentence *Their mothers are at the supermarket*, the prepositional phrase *at the supermarket* is an Adverbial of place. Most adverbials are optional; however, this one cannot be left out, otherwise the sentence makes no sense, i.e. *\*Their mothers are*. Most adverbials are also typically mobile; however, this compulsory adverbial cannot be moved about: *\*At the supermarket, their mothers are.*

## Object Complement (Co)

**Object Complements** (Co) complete the clause by giving information about the Object or what the Object has been made to do. Object Complements tend to pair with complex-transitive verbs:

22a. *Janet **made** Jimmy Teacher of the Year.*
    S    V    O        Co

22b. *Janet **made** Jimmy give a speech.*
    S    V    O        Co

Notice that, in either of the above, the sentence will not be complete without the Co: *\*Janet made Jimmy*. Hence, the noun phrase *Teacher of the Year* and the non-finite subordinate clause *give a speech* are obligatory participants.

Complements can take the following forms:

| Noun Phrase | He is [a great teacher]. |
|---|---|
| Adjective Phrase | They consider that lecturer [very crazy]. |
| Finite Subordinate Clause | I am [who she wants me to be]. |
| Non-finite Subordinate Clause | She made him [look like a fool]. |

## Adverbial

Adverbials tell us the circumstances in which the actions and processes being described by the clause or sentence occurred. Adverbials generally correspond to these question words: where, when, why, how, etc. Take note that Adverbial is a function label, while adverb is a word-class label.

Adverbials are constituents that modify the verbs in clauses. They are usually optional, and it is possible for there to be several Adverbials in a clause:

23. *Jennifer* *calmly* **sat** *on that chair* *yesterday*.
    S       A       V        A           A

Prepositional phrases can function as adverbials or postmodifiers of head nouns, and sometimes it may be difficult to tell them apart. If a prepositional phrase is an *adverbial*, it tells us something about the verb: it is typically optional and/or it is mobile, i.e. it can be moved around in the sentence:

*Mom cut the vegetables.*
*Mom cut the vegetables* *with a sharp knife*.
*With a sharp knife*, *Mom cut the vegetables.*

> If the prepositional phrase functions as a postmodifier to the head noun, it is not mobile, i.e. it cannot be moved around because of its close relationship to the head noun:
>
> *Mom needed the vegetables <u>in the freezer</u>.*
> *<u>In the freezer</u>, Mom needed the vegetables.*

### Grammar Detective

Identify the underlined structures in the sentences below according to both the form and function. Form refers to the word class, names of phrases and clauses. Function refers to the specific role that the structure plays in the sentence – S, V, O, C, A, premodifier or postmodifier of head noun, and head of noun phrase.

i.      She found the students <u>very disciplined</u>.
ii.     Research has shown that stem cells could treat incurable <u>diseases</u>.
iii.    <u>To err</u> is human.
iv.     Did you hear <u>what he said</u>?
v.      Nobody knows who <u>had tampered</u> with the car brakes.
vi.     <u>To pass Mrs Tan's test with flying colours</u> is Jonathan's goal right now.
vii.    I will meet you <u>at the playground</u> after I have completed my homework.
viii.   I offered <u>the young lady beside me</u> a magazine.
ix.     Even though the ball is made of rubber, it <u>still</u> hurts.
x.      The planner will give you expert advice <u>on planning your wedding</u>.

Adverbials can take many different forms:

| Noun Phrase | Mariah gave blood [last week]. |
|---|---|
| Prepositional Phrase | I work late [on Tuesdays and Thursdays]. |
| Adverb Phrase | She walked [very gracefully] down the steps. |
| Finite Subordinate Clause | [While we were driving to Jurong Island], we heard a loud explosion. |
| Non-finite Subordinate Clause | [To open the window], you have to climb a ladder. |

## SVOCA: How to Analyse Clause Structure

So far, we have looked at simple SVOCA analysis as well as the form and function of constituents. To help you further in analysing the SVOCA structure of clauses, follow these steps:

- First, look for all the **verbs**.
- Then identify the **verb of the main clause**.
- What **type of verb** is it? Intransitive, transitive, linking, ditransitive, complex-transitive?
- Ask yourself: Who is doing what, to whom, under what circumstances? – determine the number of **participants**.
- Do the phrases and clauses group to form bigger standalone meaningful chunks, i.e. **constituents**? One way to test for constituency is to substitute each constituent with a question word (*who, what, where, when, why, how* etc.) or with a pronoun (*it, s/he, they* etc.)
- Label **V** first, then **S**, **O**, **Oi**, **Od**, **Cs**, **Co**, **A**. Check that constituents are clearly segmented, for example, | S | V | O | A | Oi | Od |. There should be only one set of SVOCA for each main clause.
- Indicate ellipted (i.e. omitted) subjects in brackets in the case of coordinated clauses, e.g.:
  *She cooked and cleaned today.* = | S | V | + | and | (S=she) | V | A |

- Indicate split verb groups as "V…V", e.g.:

   *I have never given him my phone number.* = | S | V… | A | …V |

Let's take a look at some sentences and analyse their constituent structure. Consider the following sentence:

24. *Young adults who are concerned about their future will purchase insurance policies.*

There are two verbs in the sentence above: *are* and *will purchase*. The verb *are* is part of the subordinate (relative) clause *who are concerned about their future*. The main clause contains the verb phrase *will purchase*, which is a transitive verb. This means that the Verb *will purchase* requires two participants – the Subject and the Object. When we substitute the sentence with question words, we get *who* will purchase *what*:

who = *young adults who are concerned about their future*
what = *insurance policies*

This gives us the following clause structure:

| Young adults who are concerned about their future | will purchase | insurance policies |
|---|---|---|
| S | V | O |

Let's move on to another sentence:

25. *Because he is a generous person, Timmy bought his friends dessert at the restaurant yesterday.*

The verb *is* is part of the subordinate clause *Because he is a generous person*. The main verb in the sentence is the ditransitive verb *bought* which means that we need a Subject, an Indirect Object, and a Direct Object: *who bought who what*. How about the other parts of the sentence? When we substitute the entire sentence with question words, we get *why who bought who what where when*. The constituents that correspond to *why*, *where* and *when* are Adverbials:

> *why = Because he is a generous person*
> *who = Timmy*
> *who = his friends*
> *what = dessert*
> *where = at the restaurant*
> *when = yesterday*

This gives us the following clause structure:

| *Because he is a generous person,* | *Timmy* | *bought* | *his friends* | *dessert* | *at the restaurant* | *yesterday* |
|---|---|---|---|---|---|---|
| A | S | V | Oi | Od | A | A |

Now consider this sentence:

26. *Betty can always call Patrick and ask him to help her with the project.*

So what is going on in this sentence? We see three verbs – *call, ask, help*. Recall that one verb is equivalent to one clause, so there are three clauses in this sentence. Having said that, only two (out of the three) verbs are part of main, independent clauses:

Main clause 1: *Betty **can** always **call** Patrick*
Main clause 2: *and **ask** him to help her with the project*

The non-finite verb *to help* is part of a subordinate clause *to help her with the project.* Since we have two separate main clauses, we have two SVOCA structures.

In main clause 1, the Verb *can…call* requires two participants: a Subject and an Object. The adverb *always* functions as an Adverbial:

| *Betty* | *can* | *always* | *call* | *Patrick* |
|---------|-------|----------|--------|-----------|
| S | V… | A | …V | O |

The second main clause verb *ask* requires a Subject, an Object and an Object Complement. But where is the Subject in main clause 2? We know it is *Betty*, but this noun has been ellipted (i.e. omitted to avoid repetition because it is common with the first clause). As for the Verb, the auxiliary modal verb *can* has also been ellipted and the complete verb phrase is actually *can ask*. Hence, the full, complete clause is *(Betty) (can) ask him to help her with the project*:

| *and* | *(Betty)* | *(can) ask* | *him* | *to help her with the project.* |
|-------|-----------|-------------|-------|----------------------------------|
|  | (S) | V | O | Co |

Note that the conjunction *and* is a coordinating conjunction which does not get a function label, and it is not part of either clause.

Next, when dealing with questions, we need to remember that they may have a slightly different clause structure. Consider this example:

27.  *Will the teacher give John a difficult test?*

There is only one verb phrase in this sentence: *will…give*. If we consider the clause structure for the verb *give*, it is *who gives who what*, i.e. S V Oi Od:

who = *the teacher (will…give)*

who = *John*
what = *a difficult test*

Applying the constituency test to the question, this gives us:

| *Will* | *the teacher* | *give* | *John* | *a difficult test?* |
|--------|---------------|--------|--------|---------------------|
| V… | S | …V | Oi | Od |

In yes-no questions like the one above, there is always a subject-auxiliary verb inversion, so the modal auxiliary verb *will* appears before the Subject *the teacher*.

## MAIN AND SUBORDINATE CLAUSES

Based on our discussion so far, we have seen some clauses that can stand on their own, while others have to attach to main clauses, embed in main clauses or in larger phrases like noun phrases.

### Main (Independent) Clauses

**Main clauses** are also known as **independent clauses**. They can stand on their own as a sentence. They contain finite verbs or verb phrases, and they must have subjects:

28.  *She borrowed my pen.*

This sentence has the clause structure SVO, and the Verb *borrowed* is finite.

Sometimes, when main clauses are coordinated with conjunctions like *and* or *but*, subjects may be ellipted (omitted in order to avoid repetition) as shown by Ø below:

29.  *She borrowed my pen and Ø completed her homework with it.*

In the sentence above, there are two finite verbs (*borrowed* and *completed*) and hence two clauses: (i) *She borrowed my pen* and (ii) *(She) completed her homework with it.*

Earlier, it was mentioned that main clauses contain finite verbs and must have subjects. There is however, one exception to this – the imperative verb which is used to give an order or instruction, or to make a request:

30.  *Complete your homework!*

There is no subject in the sentence, and hence, the verb *complete* is non-finite (because there is nothing the verb has to agree with).

## Subordinate/Dependent/Embedded clauses

**Subordinate clauses** are also known as **dependent clauses** and they include **embedded clauses.** These clauses cannot stand on their own and they have to attach to other clauses, or be embedded within bigger clauses and, sometimes, in noun phrases too. Overt subjects are not a requirement: some subordinate clauses have subjects, while others do not. When there is no subject, the subordinate clause typically contains a non-finite verb. Some examples are given below, with the subordinate clauses underlined:

31.  *If you **are** dissatisfied with their service, you can file a complaint.*
32.  *Susan was late for the exam because she **missed** her bus.*
33.  ***Baking** cookies is my favourite pastime.* (non-finite verb in subordinate clause)
34.  *Houses **overlooking** the lake cost more.* (non-finite verb in embedded clause)

## Combining clauses

To form longer or more complex sentences, we can always combine clauses via coordination or subordination. **Coordination** joins main clauses together, and typically uses conjunctions such as *and, or, but, either…or* and *neither…nor*. Consider the examples below, with the main clauses underlined:

35. *<u>Samantha wanted more popcorn</u> but <u>Melissa asked for potato chips instead</u>.*
36. *<u>She cooked dinner</u> and <u>baked a cake for dessert</u>.*
37. *Either <u>we watch a movie</u> or <u>we stay at home to study</u>.*

**Subordination** or **embedding** takes place when a subordinate clause is joined to a main clause by a subordinating conjunction, or by embedding it in another clause or phrase. Subordinating conjunctions include *although, if, since, because, before, when, while, unless* and *until*. Consider the examples below (with the subordinate clauses underlined):

38. *I need a drink <u>because I am thirsty</u>.*
39. *<u>When we have no money</u>, we just watch television at home.*
40. *We will watch the movie <u>which Mary recommended</u>.*

## SENTENCE TYPES

There are four types of sentences, depending on how many clauses they contain and how the clauses are combined, i.e. whether by coordination or subordination. When we work out whether a sentence is simple, compound, complex or compound-complex, we need to look for verbs, because clauses are built around verbs. In the examples below, all main verbs are in bold.

## Simple Sentences

Simple sentences contain only one main clause – hence, there will be one main verb:

41.  *My teacher **loves** chocolate cake.*

| *My teacher* | ***loves*** | *chocolate cake.* |
|---|---|---|
| S | V | O |

## Compound Sentences

Compound sentences are made up of two or more main clauses joined by coordination. The clauses can be joined by a coordinating conjunction (*and, but, for, nor, or, so* or *yet*) or by a comma, or a semicolon. The sentence below contains two verb phrases: *do…like* and *would…like*. These verbs form two (main) clauses:

42.  *Do you want coffee, or would you like tea instead?*

| ***Do…*** | *you* | ***…want*** | *coffee* |
|---|---|---|---|
| V… | S | …V | O |

| *or* | ***would…*** | *you* | ***…like*** | *tea* | *instead?* |
|---|---|---|---|---|---|
| | V… | S | …V | O | A |

## Complex Sentences

Complex sentences contain one main clause and one or more subordinate clauses. In the sentences below, the subordinate clauses are underlined:

43. *The students **are studying** <u>because they **have** a test tomorrow.</u>*

| The students | are studying | because they have a test tomorrow. |
|:---:|:---:|:---:|
| S | V | A |

44. *Houses **overlooking** <u>the lake</u> **are** very expensive.*

| Houses overlooking the lake | are | very expensive. |
|:---:|:---:|:---:|
| S | V | Cs |

Dependent clauses are introduced by these subordinate conjunctions, or relative pronouns:

## Subordinating Conjunctions

| after | because | since | until |
|:---:|:---:|:---:|:---:|
| although | before | so | when |
| as | even if | so that | whenever |
| as if | even though | than | where |
| as long as | how | that | wherever |
| as soon as | if | though | whether |
| as though | in order that | unless | while |

## Relative Pronouns

| who | whom | whose | which | that |
|:---:|:---:|:---:|:---:|:---:|

## Compound-Complex Sentences

Compound-complex sentences are a mix of both coordination (compound sentences) and subordination/embedding (complex sentences). There are at least two main/independent clauses and one or more subordinating/dependent clauses.

The subordinate clauses are underlined in the examples below:

45. *When the bell **rang**, the students **ran** to their seats and the teacher **started** her lesson.*

| When the bell rang, | the students | *ran* | to their seats |
|---|---|---|---|
| A | S | V | A |

| and | the teacher | *started* | her lesson. |
|---|---|---|---|
| | S | V | O |

46. ***Update** us often and **tell** us how you're **coping**.*

| *Update* | us | often |
|---|---|---|
| V | O | A |

| and | *tell* | us | how you're coping. |
|---|---|---|---|
| | V | Oi | Od |

Note that the coordinating conjunction *and* above joins main clauses, while the subordinate clauses involve subordinating conjunction like *when* and embedding within another clause. Also note that the SVOCA structures in *Update us often and tell us how you're coping* do not contain Subjects. This is because these involve (non-finite) imperative verbs, which do not take Subjects.

## Grammar Detective

For each sentence below, identify the clausal structure (i.e. SVOCA) of each main clause, labelling each constituent and indicating elipted elements clearly. Indicate what type of sentence it is.

Example:

*The book that Jonathan read is on the shelf.*

**Type of sentence**: complex sentence

| *The book Jonathan read* | *is* | *on the shelf.* |
|---|---|---|
| S | V | A |

i.   I wanted the Nintendo but Mom got me a writing set.

ii.  Some students can remember the coordinating conjunctions but others can only remember their favourite pizza toppings.

iii. This year, after a lengthy, noisy debate, they decided on the guest list.

iv.  I did not see them at the station because Mary and Samantha arrived at the bus station before noon.

v.   John went to school, but James remained at home because he had a fever.

vi.  Jimmy headed for home quickly and quietly.

vii. Was she ever in a storm that was full of lightning, or doesn't she recall?

viii. Seeing how much you dislike durians makes me sad.

ix.  Solving equations is useful, but studying grammar is fun.

x.    The worksheet is where you have put it.

xi.   When the play ended, the curtain closed, and the audience applauded.

xii.  Sylvia hit the dirty old man in the face with her purse.

## SENTENCE FORM AND FUNCTION

Sentences of English may take four different forms depending on the word order: declarative, interrogative, imperative and exclamatory. When a speaker uses these sentence forms for different purposes, we then refer to the sentence functions: statements, questions and commands/requests.

## Declarative Sentences

| | |
|---|---|
| Form: | Declarative sentences typically have the word order Subject Verb (SV). |
| Function: | They generally convey information or make a **statement.** |
| Example: | *Dark chocolate is good for your health.* |

## Interrogative Sentences

| | |
|---|---|
| Form: | Interrogative sentences are typically used to ask questions and may either involve the use of question words (*who, where,* etc.) or subject-auxiliary inversion (Verb comes before Subject). We put a question mark at the end of an interrogative. |
| Function: | They are typically used to seek information or to ask a **question.** |
| Example: | *What is good for your health?* (question word) / *Is dark chocolate good for your health?* (subject-auxiliary inversion) |

## Imperative Sentences

| Form: | Imperative sentences do not have any Subjects, i.e. they begin with an (imperative) verb. The subject of an imperative sentence is always understood as *you* even if it is not stated in the sentence. |
|---|---|
| Function: | In general, they are used to give **orders or commands**, and to make **requests**. |
| Example: | *Eat dark chocolate please.* |

## Exclamatory Sentences

| Form: | Exclamatory sentences are used to show emphasis, to express surprise or a strong emotion. They end with an exclamation mark. |
|---|---|
| Function: | They are used to **emphasise** something. |
| Example: | *I cannot believe dark chocolate is good for my health!* |

In summary, we saw how clauses are structured around verbs in this chapter. We learnt how to analyse the structure of a clause and how to identify the function of each constituent. Finally, we looked at different types of clauses and sentences.

## Direct speech

"I'll see you tomorrow."

**Friday afternoon**

## Indirect / Reported speech

"The teacher told the students (that) she would see them the next day."

**Sunday**

# CHAPTER SIX

# VARIATIONS IN SENTENCE STRUCTURE

In Chapter 5, we learnt how sentences are formed by combining clauses, and we looked at four sentence types: simple, compound, complex and compound-complex. In this chapter, we will explore the variations in sentence structures – how we vary our sentences and connect events together in different ways to give focus to different elements in our sentences.

## Active vs Passive Sentences

Sentences can be active or passive. A sentence in the **active voice** has the **agent** or **doer** of the action in the subject position (remember that the word order in English is generally SVO, or Subject-Verb-Object):

1.  *The brave mouse <u>chased</u> the timid cat.*

| Subject | Verb | Object |
|---|---|---|
| *The brave mouse* | *chased* | *the timid cat.* |
| mouse: agent (doer of the action) | | cat: patient (or undergoer) of the action |

In this active sentence, the agent or doer of the action *chased* is *the brave mouse*, and *the timid cat* is the patient or undergoer of the action.

In the **passive voice**, the **patient (or undergoer)** of the action appears at the beginning of the sentences and functions as the subject of the sentence. The **BE passive auxiliary** (below, *was*) is used to form the passive verb form, and the agent or doer of the action appears in a *by*-phrase, functioning as an adverbial:

2.    *The timid cat <u>was chased</u> by the brave mouse.*

| Subject | Verb | Adverbial |
|---------|------|-----------|
| *The timid cat* | *was chased* | *by the brave mouse.* |
| cat: patient (or undergoer) of the action | (BE passive auxiliary) | mouse: agent (doer of the action) |

In the active voice, the subject of the sentence is seen as actively carrying out the action described, and in the passive voice, the subject is passively undergoing the action. When we use the active sentence, we focus on the agent/doer, i.e. we foreground the doer of the action by placing it at the beginning of the sentence. Passive sentences allow us to avoid mentioning the agent, as seen in the sentence below. This is useful especially when we want to focus on the patient, or when we are not certain who/what was the agent/doer of the action.

3.    *The timid cat <u>was chased</u>.*

| Subject | Verb |
|---------|------|
| *The timid cat* | *was chased* |
| cat: patient (or undergoer) of the action | (BE passive auxiliary) |

In spoken English, we sometimes use the *get*-passives: *She <u>invited</u> us to her party. / We <u>got invited</u> to her party.*

Here are some examples of active and passive sentences with different verb forms:

| Verb Forms | Active | Passive |
|---|---|---|
| Simple present | Sally _cleans_ the room every weekend. | The room _is cleaned_ (by Sally) every weekend./The room _is cleaned_ every weekend (by Sally). |
| Simple past | Sally _cleaned_ the room yesterday. | The room _was cleaned_ (by Sally) yesterday. |
| Present progressive/continuous | Sally _is cleaning_ the room. | The room _is being cleaned_ (by Sally). |
| Past progressive/continuous | Sally _was cleaning_ the room when her sister called out for help. | The room _was being cleaned_ (by Sally) when her sister called out for help. |
| Present perfect | Sally _has cleaned_ the room. | The room _has been cleaned_ (by Sally). |
| Past perfect | Sally _had cleaned_ the room before her sister called out for help. | The room _had been cleaned_ (by Sally) before her sister called out for help. |
| Future with modal verb _will_ | Sally _will clean_ the room next weekend. | The room _will be cleaned_ (by Sally) next weekend. |
| Future with modal verb _would_ | Sally _would clean_ the room if she had more free time. | The room _would be cleaned_ by Sally if she had more free time./ The room _would be cleaned_ if Sally had more free time. |

Have you noticed that you cannot transform some active sentences into passive sentences? For instance, it is not possible to convert the active sentence *The children walked to the store* or *Mr Tan became a principal* into a passive. Why is this so? Only verbs that take objects can be passivised. In other words, only sentences with transitive, ditransitive and complex-transitive verbs can be transformed from actives into passives.

In the example *The children walked to the store*, the verb *walked* is an intransitive verb which does not take any object. The prepositional phrase *to the store* functions as an adverbial. In *Mr Tan became a principal,* the verb is a linking verb which also does not take an object – the noun phrase *a principal* is a complement.

## Grammar Detective

Determine whether the sentences below are active or passive. If they are active, convert them to passive and if they are in the passive voice, convert them to active. For the passive sentences, you may have to come up with your own agent/ doer of the verb.

i.    The children spotted a very strange animal in the forest.
ii.   She should not feed the animals at the zoo.
iii.  Chinese is said to be a difficult language.
iv.   John gave his wife a bouquet of flowers.

v.    Those letters must have been written by that disgruntled employee.

vi.   That patient teacher always answers all her students' questions.

vii.  They appointed Jasper class chairman.

viii. Someone received an emergency call late last night.

ix.   Millions of dollars are being wasted on the new controversial programme every year.

x.    Iman's mother hides money in the kitchen.

## Think about the voice...

*Bielenda Extra Energy Face Cream for Men effectively eliminates signs of fatigue caused by lack of sleep, stress, or unhealthy lifestyles. It gives the skin vitality and strength, and strengthens its resistance to harmful external factors. Bielenda repairs the epidermis. Used in the morning, Bielenda boosts skin energy and vitality for the whole day. It also helps to maintain a proper level of hydration of the skin during shaving, and accelerates the regeneration of microdamages incurred during shaving.*

Have you noticed how this text makes use of the active voice extensively? Why do you think this is the case?

Here are some of the reasons to use the passive voice:
- The agent (doer) of the action is unimportant:
  *The pyramids <u>were built</u> a long time ago.*
- The agent is unknown:
  *Several accidents <u>were reported</u> during the storm last night.*

- The agent is common knowledge, and mentioning it would be redundant:
  *Barack Obama <u>was elected</u> in 2008.*
- The writer desires to control focus of sentence:
  i) to emphasise the party (Jack) receiving the action:
  *Jack <u>was kicked</u> by Jill.*
  ii) to de-emphasise the agent's role in the action:
  *The alarm <u>was triggered</u> by my son.*
  Compare the use of the passive verb with the active:
  *One million Tutsis <u>were killed</u> in the Rwandan civil war.*
  vs
  *Hutus <u>killed</u> one million Tutsis in the Rwandan civil war.*

## Direct vs Indirect/Reported Speech

When we use **direct speech**, we repeat exactly what someone has said, using the words the person used. Direct speech is placed inside quotations marks, with the first word inside the quotation marks beginning with a capital letter. **Reported speech**, also known as **indirect speech**, reports what others said. We use reported speech when we want to focus on the content of what someone said instead of their exact words. No quotation marks are used to enclose what the person said in reported speech.

## Changing Verb Forms

When transforming sentences from direct speech to indirect speech, we may need to change verb forms (especially related to tense), personal pronouns, and references to time and place.

### No change in present tense verb forms

In reported speech, when the reporting, or saying, verb is in the present tense, we do not change the tense:

| Direct Speech | | Indirect/Reported Speech |
|---|---|---|
| Simple present<br>*Marianne exclaims, "I love durians!"* | no change | *Marianne exclaims (that) she loves durians.* |
| Factual statements<br>*My teacher taught me, "The earth is round."* | | *My teacher taught me (that) the earth is round.* |

The subordinate clause in the reported speech can optionally be introduced by the conjunction *that,* as in the second example above.

**Change present verb forms to the past tense**

Sometimes when we transform direct speech to reported speech, we need to change the verb in the direct quote from present tense to past tense forms. This happens when the reporting verbs, i.e. *told, exclaimed, said* and *shared,* in the examples below, are in the past tense:

| Direct Speech | | Indirect/Reported Speech |
|---|---|---|
| **Simple present**<br>*"I love you," John told Mary.* | change to | *John told Mary (that) he loved her.* |
| **Present progressive/ continuous**<br>*Janet exclaimed, "The robber is running across the field!"* | | *Janet exclaimed (that) the robber was running across the field.* |
| **Present perfect**<br>*"The rain has stopped," said Mary.* | | *Mary said (that) the rain had stopped.* |
| **Present perfect progressive/ continuous**<br>*Albert shared, "I have been eating all day."* | | *Albert shared (that) he had been eating all day.* |

## Change past verb forms to past perfect forms

There are also changes to the past verb forms as seen below:

| Direct Speech | | Indirect/Reported Speech |
|---|---|---|
| **Simple past**<br>*"I met her at the mall," John shared.* | change<br>to | *John shared (that) he <u>had met</u> her at the mall.* |
| Past progressive/continuous<br>*"I was dreaming about my party," claimed Mary.* | | *Mary claimed (that) she <u>had been dreaming</u> about her party.* |

## Change imperatives to *to*-infinitive forms

When the direct quote is an imperative, we transform the verb from an imperative to an infinitive as seen in the examples below:

| Direct Speech | | Indirect/Reported Speech |
|---|---|---|
| *Linda reminded me, "Please take care of your puppy."* | change<br>to | *Linda reminded me <u>to take care of</u> my puppy.* |
| *Jimmy shouted at me, "Don't slice the apple!"* | | *Jimmy shouted at me not <u>to slice</u> the apple.* |

## Change some modal verb forms

When the verb in the direct quote begins with a modal which functions as the present tense form, then we change this to the past tense equivalent in reported speech:

| Direct Speech | | Indirect/Reported Speech |
|---|---|---|
| *"I will meet you at 8pm," said John.* | change<br>to | *John said (that) he <u>would</u> meet her at 8pm.* |
| *Mary told Tom, "The train may be late."* | | *Mary told Tom (that) the train <u>might</u> be late.* |

| | | |
|---|---|---|
| *He warned, "It might rain later."* | no change, since *might* and *should* here are past modal forms | *He warned (that) it <u>might</u> rain later.* |
| *"You should relax," said the doctor.* | | *The doctor said (that) I <u>should</u> relax.* |

## Changing Pronouns and Possessive/Demonstrative Determiners

When we transform direct speech into reported speech, we also change first and second person pronouns and possessive determiners to third person pronouns/determiners in reported speech:

| Direct Speech | | Indirect/Reported Speech |
|---|---|---|
| *"I like ice cream," declared John.* | change to | *John declared (that) <u>he</u> liked ice cream.* |
| *The sisters told Willy, "We enjoyed your singing."* | | *The sisters told Willy (that) <u>they</u> had enjoyed <u>his</u> singing.* |
| *"He wants this book," shared Mary.* | | *Mary shared (that) he wanted <u>that</u> book.* |

Remember to make changes to the verb forms too, as discussed in the earlier section, **Changing Verb Forms**.

## Changing the References to Time and Place (Adverbials of Time and Place)

One other change takes place when we change direct speech to reported speech – some adverbs/ adverbials of time and place must change:

| Direct Speech | | Indirect/Reported Speech |
|---|---|---|
| *here, today, yesterday, next week, last year* etc. | | *there, that day, the previous day/the day before, the following week/the week after, the previous year* etc. |
| *"We're leaving now," said Jimmy.* | change to | *John said (that) they were leaving <u>then</u>.* |
| *"We'll see you tomorrow," the teachers told the students.* | | *The teachers told the students (that) they would see them <u>the next day</u>.* |

## Transforming Questions in Direct Speech to Reported Speech

When transforming questions from direct speech to indirect speech, we need to make subject-auxiliary inversion, in addition to other required changes involving tenses, pronouns, determiners and references to time and place.

### Change yes-no questions to reported speech

When we change direct speech involving yes-no questions to reported speech, we introduce the subordinate clause with the conjunctions *if* or *whether*. There is also an auxiliary and subject inversion.

| Direct Speech | | Indirect/Reported Speech |
|---|---|---|
| *He asked, "Are there any chairs in the room?"* | | *He asked <u>whether</u> **there were** any chairs in the room.* |
| *He enquired, "Is there a concert this evening?"* | change to | *He enquired <u>if</u> **there was** a concert that evening.* |
| *"Can you speak Japanese?" she asked me.* | | *She asked me <u>if</u> **I could** speak Japanese.* |

### Change wh-questions to reported speech

When transforming wh-questions in direct speech to reported speech, we use the following structure: reporting/asking verb + question word + clause. We apply subject-auxiliary inversion and make the other required changes to verb tenses and pronoun/determiners. The reported speech is also referred to as indirect questions.

| Direct Speech | | Indirect/Reported Speech |
|---|---|---|
| *The principal asked the student, "Where are you going?"* | change to | *The principal asked the student <u>where</u> **she was going**.* |
| *"When **will** you buy the concert ticket?" asked Ramli.* | | *Ramli asked <u>when</u> **I would buy** the concert ticket.* |

Have you also noticed the changed punctuation marks in all the examples we have discussed so far? Pay close attention to the punctuation marks inside the direct quote and after the reporting/saying verb, as well as those at the end of sentences.

**Direct speech:** "You need to relax," the doctor told me. / The doctor told me, "You need to relax."

**Indirect/reported speech:** The doctor told me (that) I needed to relax.

## Grammar Detective

Rewrite the direct speech as indirect/reported speech.

i.   Maisy told me, "I lost my favourite necklace during my birthday party."

ii.  "Sit down now!" the principal shouted at the class.

iii. "Is this the way to the train station?" asked the tourist.

iv.  "I want all the tigers in the village to be killed by next week," the angry king bellowed.

v.   Daisy reminded her students, "You can start working on your projects tomorrow."

CHAPTER SEVEN

# SUBJECT-VERB AGREEMENT

In Chapter 4, we looked at the different types of verbs. In this chapter, we will explore the notion of subject-verb agreement – where the verb agrees with the subject, specifically the head noun in the subject position.

## Singular vs Plural Nouns

In finite clauses, subject-verb agreement refers to the relationship between the noun in the subject position and the verb. When the noun in the subject position is singular, the verb is also singular:

1.  _This student_     _loves_    chocolate.
        singular      singular
      noun/subject     verb

    but NOT
    * _This student love chocolate._

When the noun is plural, the verb changes accordingly:

2.  _Many students_   _love_    chocolate.
       plural        plural

noun/subject          verb
  but NOT
* *Many students loves chocolate.*

Plural nouns are marked by the plural *-s.* The same rule also applies to irregular nouns like *person/people* and *child/children.*

There are some uncountable nouns that end with an *-s* like *news, economics, linguistics, mathematics, mumps.* In these instances, these nouns must take singular verbs:

*Today's news <u>is</u>/*are really interesting.*
*The news <u>needs</u>/*need to be at an earlier time for me to watch it.*

English also has nouns which are inherently plural; these nouns do not have a singular form. What makes these (inherently) plural nouns difficult to identify is that they do not end with the plural marker *-s.* Some examples include *police, cattle, youth.*

*The police <u>are</u> here. Look at the number of police cars and policemen!*
*\*The police is here. Look at the number of police cars and policemen!*

*The cattle <u>are</u> grazing on the farmer's fertile land.*
*The sick <u>are</u> to be cared for at home.*

## Conjoined Nouns and Noun Phrases

When the subject consists of two or more nouns/noun phrases connected by *and*, it would typically take a plural verb, e.g. <u>*A computer* and *a printer*</u> **are** *important tools for the office.* However, it should be noted that sometimes nouns joined by the conjunction *and* are used to denote a single idea, and so a singular verb is required, as seen in these examples:

3.    <u>*Sausages and eggs*</u> **is** *Jason's favourite breakfast.*
4.    <u>*Fish and chips*</u> **is** *commonly eaten in England.*

It is possible to consider *fish* and *chips* as two separate food items (instead of seeing it as one type of dish), and then a plural verb must follow: *Fish and chips <u>are</u> a marriage made in heaven.*

### *Either…or* and *neither…nor*

Sometimes nouns/noun phrases are joined by *either…or* or *neither…nor.*

- When <u>two singular subjects</u> are connected by *either…or* or *neither …nor,* they take a singular verb:

5.    *Either <u>a boy</u> or <u>a girl</u>* **has** *to go down to the office now.*

- When <u>two plural subjects</u> are connected by *either…or* or *neither …nor,* they take a plural verb:

6.    *Neither <u>the boys</u> nor <u>the girls</u>* **have** *to go down to the office now.*

- When the subject is comprised of a singular and a plural noun phrase, then, the proximity rule applies:

7.    *There is no space in the room so either <u>two chairs</u> or <u>a table</u>* **has** *got to be moved.*

The proximity rule also applies to phrases linked by *or* only, as seen in the example:

8.  *Do you think <u>these pens</u> or <u>that book</u> **is** a better gift?*

> Now try to look up "neither…nor" in one of the advanced learner's dictionaries. You will find that when two singular subjects are joined by *neither…nor,* the verb can be singular or plural — the verb is normally singular in a formal style, but can be plural in an informal style.
>
> *Neither the novel nor the poem **was** written by him.* (formal)
> *Neither the novel nor the poem **were** written by him.* (informal)
>
> Likewise, in formal style, we use the singular verb after *neither of* + noun/pronoun: *Neither of them <u>owns</u> a bicycle.* In less formal contexts, the plural verb is considered acceptable: *Neither of them <u>own</u> a bicycle.*

**A note on *either…or***

When we join two phrases or clauses with *either…or* to talk about a choice between two possibilities, we often balance the structure:

9a.  *Marianne can have either <u>cake</u> or <u>muffins</u>.* (nouns)
10a.  *Jonathan is either <u>in his room</u> or <u>in the kitchen</u>.* (prepositional phrases)
11a.  *Either <u>you prepare the ingredients tonight</u> or <u>you will have to cook in a hurry tomorrow morning</u>.* (clauses)

The above structures are considered standard and formal. Unbalanced sentences are becoming common, though some choose to avoid them:

9b.   *Marianne can either <u>have cake</u> or <u>muffins</u>.*
10b. *Jonathan is either <u>in his room</u> or <u>the kitchen</u>.*
11b. *You either <u>prepare the ingredients tonight</u> or <u>you will have to cook in a hurry tomorrow morning</u>.*

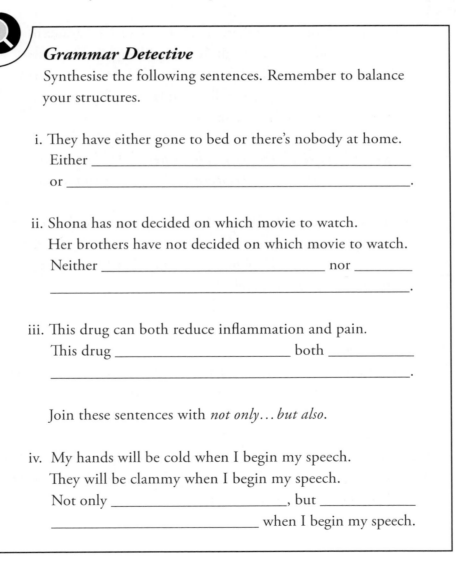

### Grammar Detective

Synthesise the following sentences. Remember to balance your structures.

i. They have either gone to bed or there's nobody at home.
   Either _____
   or _____.

ii. Shona has not decided on which movie to watch.
    Her brothers have not decided on which movie to watch.
    Neither _____ nor _____
    _____.

iii. This drug can both reduce inflammation and pain.
     This drug _____ both _____
     _____.

Join these sentences with *not only… but also.*

iv. My hands will be cold when I begin my speech.
    They will be clammy when I begin my speech.
    Not only _____, but _____
    _____ when I begin my speech.

## Uncountable Nouns

In Chapter 3, we learnt that uncountable nouns like *information, rice, sugar* refer to things that cannot be counted. We also identified different properties of uncountable nouns – generally, they do not have plural forms (*\*rices*); they are considered grammatically singular (*Rice is expensive*); and if we need to "count" uncountable nouns, we use them with *partitives* like *two bowls of rice*.

What about conjoined uncountable nouns, i.e. when we join two uncountable nouns like *flour* and *butter* with the coordinating conjunction *and*? Consider these examples:

12. *How much butter **is** needed?* (singular verb)
13. *How much flour **is** needed?* (singular verb)
14. *How much butter and flour **are** needed?* (plural verb)
15. *How much butter and flour mixture **is** needed?* (singular verb, because the verb agrees with the head noun, mixture)

When we have conjoined uncountable nouns like *butter and flour*, this noun phrase is considered plural, and requires a plural verb to follow. Other examples include *Running and swimming **are** my favourite sports*, but when we include another noun to function as the head of the noun phrase, then the verb may change from plural to singular, as seen in this example: *Performance in running and swimming **is** enhanced by eating chocolate cake before each training session.*

## Collective Nouns

We also learnt about collective nouns like *team* and *family* in Chapter 3. If you can recall, a collective noun refers to a group of people or animals as a unit. The members of that group could act together as one or as separate individuals, and may take a singular verb or a plural verb accordingly. If the emphasis is on the group acting as a single unit, a singular verb is used:

16a. _The jury_ **agrees** _that the prosecutor did not provide enough evidence._

17a. _The committee's_ _decision_ **is** _unanimous._

A plural verb is used if the members that make up the group are acting as separate members, with separate ideas and decisions:

16b. _The jury_ **were** _divided in their decisions and could not submit a verdict._

17b. _The committee_ **have** _been disagreeing with each other since their first meeting._

## Amounts and Quantities

Care should be taken with plural subjects that refer to time, distances, heights, weights or amounts of money (amounts and quantities). If they represent a single sum or quantity, a singular verb should be used:

18. _Ten years_ **is** _quite a long time to be engaged._

19. _A million dollars_ **is** _a lot of money._

20. _Five kilograms_ of sugar **costs** _$4.00._

21. _Ten kilometres_ **is** _quite a distance to run._

## Indefinite Pronouns

In Chapter 3, we looked at the different types of pronouns, including indefinite pronouns.

- Some indefinite pronouns are considered singular: _each, either, neither, one, another, much, anybody, anyone, somebody, someone, everybody, everyone, nobody, no one._ When we pair these indefinite pronouns with a verb, the verb is also singular:

22. _Nobody_ **is** _going to the party._/_No one_ **is** _going to the party._

23. _Either of these proposals_ **is** _acceptable._/_Either_ **is** _acceptable._

- Other indefinite pronouns are plural: *both, few, several, many.* They take plural verbs:

24. <u>Both</u> **are** *acceptable.*
25. <u>Few</u> **have** *supported the new initiative.*

- There are some indefinite pronouns like *all, more, most, some,* and *none* that can take both a singular or plural verb:

26. <u>Some</u> *of the water* **has** *been consumed.*/<u>Some</u> **has** *been consumed.*
27. <u>Most</u> *of the errors* **have** *been corrected.*/<u>Most</u> **have** *been corrected.*

The difference between the two examples above lies in the type of head noun found in the two noun phrases. When the head noun is uncountable like *water,* the verb is singular, and when the head noun is countable and plural like *errors,* the verb is plural too. However, when the head noun is countable and singular, the verb is singular, as seen in:

28. *Some of the <u>pie</u>* **is** *missing.*
29. *Some of the <u>pies</u>* **are** *missing.*

The same type of subject agreement rules apply to other expressions that show "parts" like *half of, three quarters of, twenty percent of, a percentage of, two-fifths of,* etc. They take:

» A **singular verb** when they are used with <u>an uncountable noun</u> like *Three quarters of the <u>flour</u>* **has** *been used.*
» A **plural verb** when they are used with <u>a plural countable noun</u> like *Three quarters of the <u>projects</u>* **have** *been completed.*
» A **singular verb** when they are used to refer to <u>a portion of a single countable noun</u> like *Three quarters of the <u>project</u>* **has** *been completed.*

## As Well As...

Nouns accompanied by a phrase beginning with *like, as well as, with, along with, together with, in addition to,* are not affected by these words. The verb used should agree with the subject of the sentence only. These phrases introduced by *as well as, along with, together with* are typically marked by a pair of commas, and serve to provide additional information about the subject. Although these expressions seem to have meanings that are similar to the conjunction *and,* they are grammatically different. In the sentences below, the verb agrees with the subjects *Jimmy* and *Peter* only:

30. *Jimmy,* as well as Jenny, **is** an artist.
    (subject)

31. *Peter,* with several others, ***has been given*** a reward.
    (subject)

## *One of ...* + **Relative Clause**

Consider these two sentences and note the difference between them (clue: look at the verbs):

32. <u>*One of the teachers*</u> **inspires** *students in the school.*
33. *Mrs Lim is one of the <u>teachers</u> who* **inspire** *students in the school.*

In 32, the singular verb *inspires* is used because the subject is singular, i.e. in the noun phrase *one of the teachers,* the head noun is *one.* When we consider how many teachers inspire students, only one does. In 33, we find the plural verb *inspire* because the verb agrees with the head noun *teachers.* When we consider the meaning of the second sentence, we get: some teachers inspire students in the school, and Mrs Lim is one of them. Why is this so?

Consider the clause structure of the sentence *Mrs Lim is one of the teachers who* **inspire** *students in the school*:

| Mrs Lim | is | one of the teachers who inspire students in the school |
|---|---|---|
| S | V | Cs |

The subject complement *one of the teachers who inspire students in the school* takes the form of a noun phrase. The head noun in that noun phrase is *one*:

| Head Noun | Prepositional phrase functioning as post-modifier to the head noun |
|---|---|
| *one* | *of the teachers who inspire students in the school* |

When we only consider the noun phrase embedded within the prepositional phrase above, we find that the verb in the relative clause must agree with the head noun *teachers*:

| Determiner functioning as pre-modifier to head noun | Head Noun | Relative clause functioning as post-modifier to the head noun |
| :---: | :---: | :--- |
| *the* | *teachers* | *who **inspire** students in the school* |

## Agreement in Existential Sentences

An *existential sentence* is a sentence that asserts the existence (or nonexistence) of something. For this purpose, English relies on constructions introduced by the adverb *there*. In terms of agreement, even though *there* is in the subject position, the verb agrees in number with the noun phrase (the head noun of a noun phrase to be precise) that comes after the verb:

34a. *There is a hardworking student in this class.*
35a. *There are some hardworking students in this class.*

In the example above, we see that the verb agrees with the head noun *student* or *students* which come after the verb, and not with the subject of the sentence *there*. Why is this the case? This is because they are said to have come from these sentences:

34b. *A hardworking student is in this class.*
35b. *Some hardworking students are in this class.*

### Grammar Detective

Try out this activity on subject-verb agreement. Find the most appropriate verb for each sentence.

i.  "The police _____ here!" the burglars exclaimed in unison when they saw the police cars that had arrived.
    (a)  is              (c)  was
    (b)  are             (d)  were

ii. "All the work _____ been done, teacher!" said Desmond.
    (a)  has             (c)  had
    (b)  have            (d)  is having

iii. "No one except his friends _____ with this brilliant idea of his," laments John.
    (a)  agree           (c)  have agreed
    (b)  agrees          (d)  had agreed

iv. Neither of the girls _____ thrilled by the news the teacher gave in class so they pulled long faces throughout their lesson yesterday.
    (a)  is              (c)  was
    (b)  are             (d)  were

v.  Neither the girls nor the boy _____ going to the class party tomorrow.
    (a)  is              (c)  was
    (b)  are             (d)  were

vi. Either Jane or the twins _____ playing with the doll when it broke.

(a)  is            (c)  was

(b)  are           (d)  were

vii. The students' executive committee _____ divided on the decision they should make in next Tuesday's meeting.

(a)  is            (c)  was

(b)  are           (d)  were

viii. "The twenty dollars you gave me _____ too little for the whole day of housework I have done," John told his mother.

(a)  is            (c)  was

(b)  are           (d)  were

ix. Measles _____ not pose a serious health problem to most people.

(a)  do            (c)  did

(b)  does          (d)  has

x.  Mr Tan, with his students, _____ the newspapers on the table right now.

(a)  weighs        (c)  is weighing

(b)  weigh         (d)  are weighing

*Grammar Detective*

Consider the following sentences. Write down the correct form of the verb in the space provided. Note that the verbs should all be in the present tense.

i.  **to have:**
    The cracked windscreen, in addition to the torn upholstery and rusted body, _____ made Ah Seng's old car very difficult to sell.

ii. **to bother:**
    Neither Ram's shabby clothes nor his sullen attitude _____ Christine, who lets Ram pick up the bill every time they dine out.

iii. **to cling:**
    Every cat hair, chocolate wrapper, and loose thread _____ to the blue pants that Tim loves to wear.

iv. **to know:**
    Any one of Dr Norhaida's students _____ the rules that govern subject-verb agreement.

v.  **to require***:*
    Mathematics _____ so much practice that Diana's poor fingers have many pen stains.

vi. **to hit:**
    Each of those singers regularly _____ notes high enough to break glass and rupture eardrums.

# Chapter Eight

# PUNCTUATION

Now that we've seen how morphemes make up words, how words make up phrases, and how phrases combine with verb phrases to form clauses and, ultimately, sentences, it's a good time to examine the little marks that help make written texts meaningful and comprehensible to the reader.

In this final chapter, we'll be taking a look at some punctuation marks in English and how to use them, paying special attention to those that concern the aspects of grammar that we've been investigating in the earlier chapters of this book.

## Punctuation and Meaning

The word *punctuation* is related to the Latin words *punctuatio* and *punctuare*, both of which have to do with the act of marking with points. Indeed, this is exactly what punctuation marks are used for in English and other languages we speak and write: to mark boundaries between phrases and clauses, and to group together sense units, so that the reader's interpretation of the text comes as close as possible to what the writer intended to convey.

Punctuation is essential to conveying meaning. Consider the well-known example below:

1.    *woman without her man is nothing*

The above string of words may be punctuated several ways, but the two examples below show how drastically different the meaning of a series of words can be with the addition of punctuation marks:

2.    *Woman, without her man, is nothing.*
3.    *Woman: without her, man is nothing.*

As can be seen, sentence 2 conveys the meaning that women are worthless, while 3 conveys the exact opposite, that men are worthless – all this with the same six words in the same order.

Before we go on to examine each punctuation mark, bear in mind that, although there are conventions in punctuation that all users of the language observe, there is also a great deal of variation depending on the writer's individual preferences, the publisher's or editor's house style, where the writer is from (for example, whether he or she follows the conventions of British English or American English) and even the age of the writer.

## Full Stop

We'll begin our discussion with the **full stop**, which is also called the **period** in American English. It is one of the most straightforward of punctuation marks to use as its main purpose is to help signal the end of a sentence.

Apart from being used at the end of sentences, full stops are also used in abbreviations. Although full stops are rarely found in abbreviations in **British English (BrE)** nowadays, they are still used a lot in **American**

**English (AmE)**, which is more conservative than BrE in many ways. The following examples illustrate the differences:

British English: *Mr, Mrs Prof, am/pm, GOP*
American English: *Mr., Mrs., Prof., a.m./p.m.* (or *A.M./P.M.*), *G.O.P.*

Some older BrE speakers do, however, still use full stops in abbreviations, except in contractions, which are abbreviations where the first and last letters of the full form are kept. Hence, *Mr* and *Mrs* would be spelt without full stops because the full forms are *Mister* and *Missus*; however, *Prof.* would require a full stop as the full form of the word, *Professor*, does not end in the letter *f*.

Full stops are used in abbreviations such as the following in AmE, and to a lesser extent in BrE:

- *e.g.* (from Latin *exempli gratia*, meaning "for example")
- *i.e.* (from Latin *id est*, meaning "that is; that is to say; in other words")
- *etc.* (from Latin *et cetera*, meaning "and so forth")

## Comma

Although the **comma** is one of the most commonly used punctuation marks, it is one of the trickiest to use, and, unsurprisingly, provokes the most debate among writers.

There are a great many uses of the comma, but let's start with the most straightforward – to mark the end of a clause or an adverbial:

4.   *When I visited Amy in India last year, she was living in Mumbai.*
5.   *Next year, I will visit her again.*

In 4, we see the use of a comma to mark the end of the subordinate clause and to signal the start of the main clause, whereas in 5, the comma marks the end of the adverbial noun phrase, and separates it from the main clause. There is a lot of variability here in that some writers would never use a comma in these examples (e.g. *Next year I will visit her again*), whereas many do.

Commas may also be used to mark out interruptions, such as when the writer makes an incidental comment or expresses an afterthought:

6a.  *The management of the railway company, <u>unsurprisingly</u>, blames the maintenance team for the breakdowns.*

7a.  *The new CEO, who, <u>it should be pointed out</u>, came from the health-care sector, has no experience in running a transport company.*

As can be seen in 6a and 7a, the commas mark out *unsurprisingly* and *it should be pointed out* as incidental comments or afterthoughts; they signal that we may pull these out of the sentences and yet the sentences would read just as naturally:

6b.  *The management of the railway company ___ blames the maintenance team for the breakdowns.*

7b.  *The new CEO, who ___ came from the healthcare sector, has no experience in running a transport company.*

The same principle is seen in the following examples:

8a.  *Mary, <u>as well as her brothers</u>, is interested in the offer.*

9a.  *Zakiah, <u>in addition to her family</u>, wants to move to a bigger place.*

10a.  *The head of engineering, <u>including his secretary</u>, has been transferred to another department.*

Note that each of the phrases *as well as her brothers*, *in addition to her family* and *including his secretary* is enclosed within commas, which signals that it may be removed without affecting the rest of the sentence as it merely provides additional information. Accordingly, in each sentence, the verb agrees with the subject, ignoring the incidental information (as we have discussed in Chapter 7):

8b. *Mary ____ is interested in the offer.*
9b. *Zakiah ____ wants to move to a bigger place.*
10b. *The head of engineering ____ has been transferred to another department.*

Although *as well as, in addition to* and *including* may have a largely similar meaning to the conjunction *and*, the fact that they are not conjunctions means that in each sentence above, the subject does not become plural, which would be the case if *and* had been used instead, e.g. *Mary and her brothers <u>are</u> interested in the offer.*

### Grammar Detective

Have a look at the following sentence. Is it correct? If it isn't, why do you think it is wrong?

*That's the salesman whom I think cheated my friend last year.*

This brings us to the use of commas in relative clauses. As we've already discussed in Chapter 3, there are two kinds of relative clauses: non-restrictive (also called non-defining) and restrictive (also called defining). Have a look at the sentences below:

11. *Ben's boss, <u>who likes wine</u>, always buys several bottles from our store.*
12. *Ben's colleague <u>who speaks fluent Korean</u> was asked to be interpreter.*

In 11, the relative clause *who likes wine* is set off with commas, meaning that it may be removed from the sentence without affecting its meaning. Indeed, since Ben almost certainly has only one boss, there is no need to define which boss we're talking about; hence, the relative clause merely gives additional information about the boss and is not needed to restrict the description to a particular boss. Hence, the underlined in 11 is a non-restrictive relative clause. By contrast, in 12, since Ben almost certainly has more than one colleague, the relative clause helps to identify the colleague who was asked to be interpreter; it's the one who speaks fluent Korean. Hence, the underlined is said to be a restrictive relative clause. Note that non-restrictive relative clauses are enclosed within commas (the effect being that they may be removed from the sentence without losing any vital information), whereas restrictive relative clauses are not.

The same thing happens with noun phrases in apposition: if the second noun phrase is non-restrictive, it is enclosed within commas, but if it is restrictive, then there should not be any commas.

13. *Brenda's son, <u>Dennis</u>, is a talented flautist.*
14. *Shakespeare's play* <u>The Merchant of Venice</u> *is my favourite.*

In 13, the commas around *Dennis* suggest that it is merely additional information and that it is not needed to identify which son we are talking about; this means that Brenda has only one son. Hence, *Dennis* is non-restrictive. In 14, however, *The Merchant of Venice* is not set off with commas because it cannot be removed and is essential to the sentence; this is because Shakespeare wrote many plays, and we have to define which one we mean. Hence, *The Merchant of Venice* is restrictive.

The comma also comes in useful when one is saying something to and addressing somebody. The following is an example that some of you may be familiar with:

15a. *Let's eat Grandma.*

Without a comma, this sounds unfortunately like an invitation to eat a hapless grandmother, hence we need a comma before the term of address:

15b. *Let's eat, Grandma.*

As some people have quipped online, the comma above shows that punctuation saves lives.

As mentioned in the introduction to this section, the comma has provoked some debate among writers. Particularly controversial is the comma before the *and* or *or* in a list or a series of things, which is known as a **serial comma**. The serial comma is common in AmE, but less so in BrE, with the exception of Oxford University Press, which uses it as part of its house style, hence giving the serial comma its alternative name, the **Oxford comma**. In the example below, the last comma is a serial or Oxford comma:

16. *Peter plays the violin, viola, cello, flute, and piano.*

Although most users of BrE would not use the serial comma in the above example, using it should not be regarded as an error, but as a matter of style.

In some cases, a serial comma is helpful in making a sentence easier to read, or avoiding ambiguity. Consider the following examples:

17a. *Anushia loves British classic dishes such as fish and chips, bangers and mash and bubble and squeak.*
18a. *At the clinic yesterday, there were two babies, Dr Alfian and Dr Chai.*

If you were unfamiliar with British cuisine, you might have trouble working out how many dishes there are in 17a. Adding a comma after *mash* would signal to the reader that the second dish is bangers and mash and that the last dish is bubble and squeak. As for 18a, the suggestion seems to be that there were two babies in the clinic, and their names were Dr Alfian and Dr Chai – this is because the reader quite naturally interprets the sentence as having two noun phrases in apposition, *two babies* and *Dr Alfian and Dr Chai*. As you'll most probably agree, using a serial comma in both examples would make the above sentences a lot clearer:

17b. *Anushia loves British classic dishes such as fish and chips, bangers and mash, and bubble and squeak.*
18b. *At the clinic yesterday, there were two babies, Dr Alfian, and Dr Chai.*

## Semicolon

What punctuation mark do we use when we have two clauses and need to separate them, but a comma would be too weak a break (or wrong), and a full stop, too strong? The answer is the **semicolon**, as seen in the following sentences:

19. *Vincent got into an accident on the expressway yesterday; it was the first time he was driving alone since he passed.*
20. *Nadia tried her best to save the injured pigeon; however, it succumbed to its injuries.*

In 19, there are two main clauses which may, of course, stand on their own. There is the choice of separating them with a full stop, but this would be too strong a break, particularly since the two clauses are closely linked in meaning; in fact, the second clause serves to explain what is being narrated by the first clause. In 20, note that *however* is an adverb and not a conjunction; hence it should be preceded by either a full stop or a semicolon. Using commas in the above examples would result in what is known as a **comma splice**, which is when clauses are joined together seemingly unthinkingly using commas, and this is very much stigmatised by careful writers:

21. *Vincent got into an accident on the expressway yesterday, it was the first time he was driving alone since he passed.*

## Apostrophe

There are two main types of apostrophes. The first is the contraction apostrophe, so called because it is used to indicate an abbreviated form that had some elements omitted. The apostrophe marks the place where letters or numerals have been left out, as in the following examples:

22. *it's = it is/it has*
23. *you're = you are*
24. *don't = do not*
25. *o'clock = of the clock*
26. *fo'c's'le = forecastle*
27. *Class of '17 = Class of 2017*

When the apostrophe appears at the front of a contraction, ensure that it is curved towards the left and not to the right, which would make it a single opening quote, i.e. *'17* and not *'17*.

Apostrophes are also commonly used to show possession, e.g. *John's car* = car belonging to John. There are two points to note about the apostrophe when used to show possession. The first is that when two or more parties are mentioned and they share the possession of something, the *'s* goes at the end of the later or last party, whereas if the possession is separate, the *'s* goes at the end of each party:

28. *Henry and Annie's house is massive.* (i.e. Henry and Annie share a house.)

29. *Henry's and Annie's houses are massive.* (i.e. Henry and Annie have their own houses.)

The second point concerns nouns ending in sibilant (or hissing) sounds, such as the following:

30. *Charles's, Dickens's, Marx's, Bridget Jones's, Keats's*

The general rule is that when the addition of the possessive marker results in an additional syllable in pronunciation, then we add *'s* rather than just the apostrophe. Therefore, since we say "Charleses" and "Keatses", we spell them *Charles's* and *Keats's*. However, there are numerous exceptions to the rule. For example, the possessive forms of Classical Latin and Greek names usually have only an apostrophe added, e.g. *Herodotus', Euripides', Erasmus', Socrates', Hercules', Achilles'*. This also applies to longer English names, e.g. *St Nicholas'* and *Aloysius'*. Note also that some names do not follow the rules, and are spelt in idiosyncratic ways that have to be learnt by heart, e.g. *St James' School, Harrods, Earls Court, St Andrews* (and not, if the rules are followed, *St James's School, Harrod's, Earl's Court, St Andrew's*).

It should be pointed out that the rule above is not a hard-and-fast one; it is perfectly acceptable also to spell the first group of names as *Charles', Dickens', Marx', Bridget Jones'* and *Keats'*, but the key is to be consistent in one's practice.

# Hyphen

Hyphens have many uses, one of which is to join two or more words to indicate that they go together as a single unit. If adjective phrases are used attributively (if they come within the noun phrase, before the head noun), then they are hyphenated, and any units of measure are in the singular (this was discussed in Chapter 3):

31a.  *My teacher is a well-known author.*
32a.  *Alicia's nine-year-old son is a talent drummer.*
33a.  *The two-metre-tall basketball player cannot sit up straight in the car.*

If the adjective phrases are used predicatively (they come after a linking verb), then they are not hyphenated, and units of measure are in the plural:

31b.  *The author is well known.*
32b.  *Alicia's son is nine years old.*
33b.  *The basketball player is two metres tall.*

One notable exception to this rule is adjective phrases formed with *-ly* adverbs: these are not usually hyphenated, e.g. <u>*newly minted*</u> *professor*, <u>*poorly paid*</u> *actor*.

## Quotation Marks

Quotation marks are used to quote very short quotes (such as single words) or complete, longer quotes. Although there is a belief that single quotation marks are used for very short quotes of a word or several words, and double quotation marks for longer quotes, the real difference is that users of BrE prefer single quotation marks, whereas AmE prefers double quotation marks, e.g.:

34.  *Jon's description of his childhood as 'aimless' angered his parents. (BrE)*
35.  *Jon's description of his childhood as "aimless" angered his parents. (AmE)*

The choice of single or double quotation marks is reversed for a nested quote, or a quote within a quote:

36. *Jon said, 'My parents were angry when they found out that I had described my childhood as "aimless".' (BrE)*
37. *Jon said, "My parents were angry when they found out that I had described my childhood as 'aimless.'" (AmE)*

There is no clear preference for either single or double quotation marks in Singapore English; as always, the key is to be consistent in one's choice.

## Capitals

Finally, let's discuss the use of capital letters. They are used for proper nouns, that is, names, e.g. *Singapore, Mr Arun, Hougang, St Peter's Church*. In Singapore English, titles are also often capitalised where they would not be in BrE or AmE, e.g. *President, Chief Executive Officer, Teacher-in-Charge, Guest-of-Honour*.

Where subjects or disciplines are referred to generically, they are not capitalised; however, if they refer to names of classes, they are capitalised:

38. *During yesterday's Basic <u>Photography</u> session, we picked up some tips to improve our <u>photography</u>.*
39. *For tomorrow's Intermediate English <u>Grammar</u> class, we will be discussing the use of the subjunctive mood in English <u>grammar</u>.*

## Conclusion

In this final chapter of *The Nuts and Bolts of English Grammar*, we discussed some punctuation marks, especially those that concern the aspects of grammar examined in this book.

We hope you've enjoyed this book and learnt some useful facts about English grammar. Happy "grammaring"!

*Grammar Detective*

# SUGGESTED
# ANSWERS

## CHAPTER 1
### Page 21
Your teacher may have told you that it is ungrammatical to begin a sentence with a conjunction, such as *and* and *because*. However, when asked "Why do you like the movie?" your reply would more likely be something like "Because it stars two of my favourite actors" rather than "I like the movie because it stars two of my favourite actors", for the simple reason that it's the more natural response. And you probably also begin sentences with *and* quite often – as we have just done. Hence, we can say that the rule that it is wrong to begin sentences with *and* and *because* is prescriptive; by contrast, a descriptive grammarian would find it perfectly grammatical to do so.

## CHAPTER 2
### Page 32
*Worse* is the comparative form of the base-form adjective *bad*, and is used for comparing two people or things. However, since there are three persons in this comparison, the superlative form, *worst*, should be used instead, i.e. *the worst cook*.

### Page 38
*Drive* is a verb, which means it may be modified by an adverb. However, *safe* is an adjective rather than an adverb, so grammarians might insist on the adverb form, *safely*.

### Page 40
Conjunctions conjoin words of the same word classes, or equivalent grammatical categories. However, in the above sentence, we see *and* attempting to conjoin the adjective *tired* and a verb, *going*. Hence, an improvement would be *Joe is tired and (Joe/he) is going to bed now*, which joins two clauses, *Joe is tired* and *(Joe) is going to bed now*.

# CHAPTER 3

**Page 49**

The underlined words in the first two examples are abstract nouns. Those in the second pair are concrete nouns because they can be seen and touched.

**Page 52**

salmon → salmon

aircraft → aircraft

goose → geese

mongoose → mongooses

(computer) mouse → mouses/mice (both plural forms are accepted)

Most of these nouns take irregular plural forms, except for *mongooses* and *mouses*. One should also note the difference between *goose* and *mongoose*.

**Page 56**

| Noun | Proper vs Common | Concrete vs Abstract |
|------|------------------|----------------------|
| *family* | common | concrete |
| *home* | common | concrete |
| *spiders* | common | concrete |
| *Saturday* | proper | abstract |
| *Madam Lee* | proper | concrete |
| *sons* | common | concrete |
| *house* | common | concrete |
| *spiders* | common | concrete |
| *kitchen* | common | concrete |
| *renovation* | common | abstract |
| *works* | common | abstract |
| *species* | common | concrete |

| spider | common | concrete |
|---|---|---|
| *internet | proper?/common? | abstract?/concrete? |
| spider | common | concrete |
| enthusiasts | common | concrete |
| Trapdoor spider | proper | concrete |
| Singapore | proper | concrete |

* The *internet* is troublesome on two counts: First, it used to be treated as a name (hence spelt with a capital "I") and was thus a proper noun, but nowadays, especially in the British media, it is treated as a common noun (hence the small 'i'). Second, is the *internet* truly a physical network (i.e. concrete) or a conceptual one?

## Page 57

i. *Luggage* is uncountable in Standard English, so the plural *-s* is wrong. However, *luggages* is very common in Singapore English.

ii. *Feedback* is uncountable, but *feedbacks* is common in Singapore English.

iii. *Advice* is uncountable, and so a singular verb *was* must follow.

iv. *E-mail*, as a variant of uncountable *mail*, should in theory also be uncountable. This is the rule that very conservative speakers of English follow. However, the countable use, *e-mails*, is so widespread (because the technology is so commonplace) that it would probably be pointless trying to insist on the uncountable use.

v. *Three coffees* is not wrong; in fact it's idiomatic English. Native speakers would find this much more natural than *three cups of coffee* in the context of placing an order.

vi. *Police* is a noun that is inherently plural. So you need a plural verb *do* to follow.

vii.   *Committee* is a typical collective noun: whether it takes a singular or plural verb depends on whether we think of it as a single unit or as several individuals acting independently. Hence, the committee *makes* a decision (as one, therefore singular), but if members disagree among each other, we need to say the committee *have* had serious disagreements (emphasis on independent individuals, hence plural).

viii.   The plural form of *deer* is *deer*; it is an irregular form.

ix.   In British English (but not American English), *team* is usually used with a plural verb (*the team are/have/*etc.), especially in sports reporting (e.g. *England are a disappointing team*). The Singapore media generally follow British usage (influenced, perhaps, by the BBC and, in particular, football commentary).

x.   *Clothing* is uncountable. *Clothes* is countable and plural. So you should use *The clothes she gave away were still in good condition.* If you must use *clothing*, then use a partitive noun like *items* to show quantity: *Please give away three items of clothing.*

## Page 62

If you looked up the word *strawberry* in a dictionary, you'll find that it's classified only as a noun. So in both examples, they are nouns. The word *strawberry* in (ii) is a premodifying noun that describes or modifies the head noun *ice cream*. A noun premodifier + head noun combination is a compound noun. The noun premodifier tells us "what kind" of head noun we have. We can often swap nouns and head nouns around, and insert a preposition: *finance minister = minister for finance.* If the noun premodifier is the material/ substance, then we get *copper kettle = kettle made of copper.* In this case, *strawberry ice cream = ice cream from strawberries/ice cream made with strawberries.*

## Page 62

The underlined words in (i) to (iv) are nouns. Remember the test where we swap premodifying nouns and head nouns around, and insert a preposition in between? *Campus poster = poster on campus.* You cannot do the same for (v): *big poster = \*poster with big/ big poster = \*poster for big.* The word *incredible* in (vi) is also not a noun – it cannot be paired with determiners like *\*This is an incredible./\*That incredible.*

## Page 64

## Page 67

   i.    My other sister hasn't sent me a postcard.

   ii.   I have only one sister.

   iii.   contains a restrictive relative clause which implies only some snakes are venomous. >> This is a true statement.

   iv.   contains a non-restrictive relative clause, separated by commas, and it implies that ALL snakes are venomous. >> This is a false statement because not all snakes are venomous.

**Page 71**

| | PREMODIFIER | | | HEAD | POSTMODIFIER |
|---|---|---|---|---|---|
| | Determiner | Adjective | Noun | | |
| 1 | | | | dolphins | |
| 2 | | | | pods | of up to a dozen individuals (Prepositional Phrase) |
| 3 | | | | places | with a high abundance of food (Prepositional Phrase) |
| 4 | | | | pods | |
| 5 | an | | | aggregation | called a superpod (Non-Finite Clause) |
| 6 | such | | | groupings | |
| 7 | a thousand | | | dolphins | |
| 8 | the | | | individuals | |
| 9 | a | | | variety | of clicks, whistles and other vocalisations (Prepositional Phrase) |
| 10 | | ultrasonic | | sounds | |
| 11 | | | | echolocation | |
| 12 | | | | membership | in pods (Prepositional Phrase) |
| 13 | | | | interchange | |
| 14 | the | | | cetaceans | |
| 15 | | strong | | bonds | between each other (Prepositional Phrase) |
| 16a | | injured, ill | | individuals | |
| 16b | | injured | | (individuals) | |
| | | ill | | individuals | |
| 17 | the | | | surface | |
| 18 | this | altruistic | | behaviour | |
| 19a | their own | | | species | |
| 19b | their | own | | species | |

Note: In Cambridge and Longman dictionaries, *own* is a determiner, but in Oxford, Collins Cobuild and Macmillan dictionaries, it is an adjective.

| 20 | *a* | | | *dolphin* | *in New Zealand (Prepositional Phrase) that goes by the name of Moko (Relative Clause)* |
| 21a | *a* | *female* | | *Pygmy Sperm Whale* | |
| 21b | *a* | *female* | *Pygmy Sperm* | *Whale* | |
| 22 | *her* | | | *calf* | |
| 23 | | *shallow* | | *water* | |

## Page 75

They are all correct. The first is informal, the second is very formal, and the last is somewhere in between in terms of formality.

  i.    *than* is used as a preposition, and prepositions take object pronouns like *me*.

  ii.   *than* is used as a conjunction which is followed by the clause *I am*, with the adjective *fast* ellipted.

  iii.  is similar to (ii), but with the verb *am* also ellipted.

# CHAPTER 4

## Page 89

  i.    finite, *-s* present tense

  ii.   finite, *-ed* past tense

  iii.  non-finite, base form (i.e. the imperative)

  iv.   non-finite, base form (i.e. the *to*-infinitive)

  v.    non-finite, *-ing* participle

  vi.   non-finite, *-ed/en* participle (i.e. the passive verb)

  vii.  non-finite, base form (i.e. the bare infinitive)

## Page 103

|     | Verb Phrase | Finiteness | Modality, Tense, Aspect | Voice |
|-----|-------------|------------|-------------------------|-------|
| i   | *visited* | F | simple past | A |
|     | *was…researching* | F | past progressive | A |
| ii  | *was…doing* | F | past progressive | A |
| iii | *is…distributed* | F | simple present | P |
|     | *has to mean* | F | simple modal | A |
|     | *are* | F | simple present | A |
| iv  | *have…developed* | F | present perfective | A |
|     | *honed* | NF | ---- | P |
| v   | *think* | NF | ---- | A |
|     | *were* | F | simple past | A |
|     | *to dispatch* | NF | ---- | A |
|     | *to train* | NF | ---- | A |

## Page 110

   i.    (d)
   ii.   (c)
   iii.  (a)
   iv.   (c)
   v.    (c)

# CHAPTER 5

## Page 126

   i.     form – adjective phrase; function – object complement
   ii.    form – noun; function – head of noun phrase
   iii.   form – non-finite subordinate clause; function – subject
   iv.    form – finite subordinate clause; function – object
   v.     form – verb phrase; function – verb
   vi.    form – non-finite subordinate clause; function – subject
   vii.   form – prepositional phrase; function – adverbial
   viii.  form – noun phrase; function – indirect object
   ix.    form – adverb; function – adverbial

x.    form – prepositional phrase; function – post-modifier to head
noun advice

## Page 137

i.

| I | wanted | the Nintendo |
|---|---|---|
| S | V | O |

| but | Mom | got | me | a writing set. |
|---|---|---|---|---|
| | S | V | Oi | Od |

ii.

| Some students | can remember | the coordinating conjunctions |
|---|---|---|
| S | V | O |

| but | others | can... | only | ...remember | their favourite pizza toppings. |
|---|---|---|---|---|---|
| | S | V... | A | ...V | O |

iii.

| This year, | after a lengthy, noisy debate, | they | decided on | the guest list. |
|---|---|---|---|---|
| A | A | S | V | O |

iv.

| I | did... | not | ...see | them | at the station | because Mary and Samantha arrived at the bus station before noon. |
|---|---|---|---|---|---|---|
| S | V... | A | ...V | O | A | A |

v.

| John | went | to school |
|------|------|-----------|
| S | V | A |

| but | James | remained | at home | because he had a sore throat. |
|-----|-------|----------|---------|-------------------------------|
| | S | V | A | A |

vi.

| Jimmy | headed | for home | quickly and quietly. |
|-------|--------|----------|----------------------|
| S | V | A | A |

vii.

| Was | she | ever | in a storm that was full of lightning |
|-----|-----|------|----------------------------------------|
| V | S | A | A |

| or | does… | n't | she | …recall? |
|----|-------|-----|-----|----------|
| | V… | A | S | …V |

viii.

| Seeing how much you dislike durians | makes | me | sad. |
|-------------------------------------|-------|----|------|
| S | V | O | Co |

ix.

| Solving equations | is | useful, |
|-------------------|----|---------|
| S | V | Cs |

| but | studying grammar | is | fun. |
|-----|------------------|----|------|
| | S | V | Cs |

x.

| The worksheet | is | where you have put it. |
|---------------|----|------------------------|
| S | V | A |

xi.

| When the play ended. | the curtain | closed |
|---|---|---|
| A | S | V |

| and | the audience | applauded. |
|---|---|---|
| | S | V |

xii.

| Sylvia | hit | the dirty old man | in the face | with her purse. |
|---|---|---|---|---|
| S | V | O | A | A |

# CHAPTER 6
## Page 145

i.   Passive: A very strange animal was spotted in the forest by the children./ A very strange animal was spotted by the children in the forest.

ii.  Passive: The animals at the zoo should not be fed (by her). You can omit "by her" since it's not quite idiomatic to say "by her".

iii. Active: They say (that) Chinese is a difficult language.

iv.  Passive: John's wife was given a bouquet of flowers by him. (also accepted) A bouquet of flowers was given to John's wife by him.

v.   Active: That disgruntled employee must have written those letters.

vi.  Passive: All her students' questions are always answered by that patient teacher.

vii. Passive: Jasper was appointed class chairman by them.

viii. Passive: An emergency call was received late last night.

ix.  Active: That new controversial programme is wasting millions of dollars every year.

x.   Money is hidden in the kitchen by Iman's mother.

Page 153

    i.     Maisy told me (that) she had lost her favourite necklace at her birthday party.

    ii.    The principal shouted at the class to sit down then.

    iii.   The tourist asked if/whether that was the way to the train station.

    iv.   The angry king bellowed (that) he wanted all the tigers in the village to be killed by the following week.

    v.    Daisy reminded her students they could start working on their projects the following/next day.

# CHAPTER 7

**Page 160**

    i.     Either <u>they have gone to bed</u> or <u>there's nobody at home</u>.

    ii.    Neither <u>Shona</u> nor <u>her brothers have decided on which movie to watch</u>.

    iii.   This drug can reduce both <u>inflammation</u> and <u>pain</u>.

    iv.   Not only <u>will my hands be cold</u>, but <u>they will also be clammy</u> when I begin my speech.

**Page 167**

    i.     (b)

    ii.    (a)

    iii.   (b)

    iv.   (c)

    v.    (a)

    vi.   (d)

    vii.  (b)

    viii. (a)

    ix.   (b)

    x.    (c)

**Page 169**

    i.    has
        *Windscreen* is the subject and it is singular.

    ii.   bothers
        The subject closer to the verb, i.e. *attitude*, matters to the subject-verb agreement.

    iii.  clings
        *Every* requires a singular verb.

    iv.  knows
        *Any one*, the subject, is singular.

    v.   requires
        *Mathematics*, a *single* area of study, requires a singular verb.

    vi.  hits
        *Each*, a singular indefinite pronoun, requires a singular verb.

# CHAPTER 8

**Page 176**

The sentence contains a noun phrase, *the salesman who cheated my friend last year*. In the relative clause, we find the interruption *I think*, which is additional information and could well have been set off with commas, or bracketed. If we remove this, we see immediately that *whom cheated my friend last year* is wrong, since the relative pronoun is the subject of the relative clause, and not the object (for the same reason, we would say *he cheated my friend last year*, and not *him cheated my friend last year*).